So Each May Learn

INTEGRATING LEARNING STYLES AND MULTIPLE INTELLIGENCES

HARVEY F. SILVER

RICHARD W. STRONG

MATTHEW J. PERINI

Association for Supervision and Curriculum Development
Alexandria, Virginia USA

®

Association for Supervision and Curriculum Development
1703 N. Beauregard St. • Alexandria, VA 22311-1714 USA
Telephone: 1-800-933-2723 or 703-578-9600 • Fax: 703-575-5400
Web site: http://www.ascd.org • E-mail: member@ascd.org

Gene Carter, *Executive Director and Chief Executive Officer*
Michelle Terry, *Deputy Executive Director, Program Development*
Nancy Modrak, *Director of Publishing*
John O'Neil, *Director of Acquisitions*
Mark Goldberg, *Development Editor*
Julie Houtz, *Managing Editor of Books*
Carolyn R. Pool, *Associate Editor*
Ernesto Yermoli, *Project Assistant*
Gary Bloom, *Director, Design and Production Services*
Georgia McDonald, *Senior Designer*
Dina Murray Seamon, *Production Coordinator*
Bob Land, *Indexer*

Printed in the United States of America.

November 2000 member book (pc). ASCD Premium, Comprehensive, and Regular members
periodically receive ASCD books as part of their membership benefits. No. FY01-02.

ASCD Product No. 100058
ASCD member price: $17.95   nonmember price: $21.95

Library of Congress Cataloging-in-Publication Data

Silver, Harvey F.
  So each may learn : integrating learning styles and multiple intelligences / Harvey F. Silver,
Richard W. Strong, and Matthew J. Perini.
      p. cm.
Includes bibliographical references and indexes.
  ISBN 0-87120-387-1 (alk. paper)
  1. Learning, Psychology of. 2. Multiple intelligences. 3. Cognitive styles. I. Title: Integrating learning
styles and multiple intelligences. II. Strong, Richard W., 1946- III. Perini, Matthew J., 1973- IV. Title.
  LB1060 .S538 2000
  370.15'2—dc21
                                        00-010876

06 05 04 03 02 01   10 9 8 7 6 5 4 3 2

So Each May Learn
Integrating Learning Styles & Multiple Intelligences

This chapter introduces Howard Gardner's theory of multiple intelligences, engages readers in self-assessment using the Silver-Strong *Multiple Intelligences Indicator,* models methods teachers employ to make use of the theory in their classrooms, and shows teachers how to analyze the types of intelligences they use in their classrooms.

This chapter introduces Carl Jung's theory of psychological types, engages educators in self-assessment using the *Learning Style Inventory for Adults,* models methods teachers use to engage learning styles in their classrooms, and shows teachers how to analyze the learning styles they use in their classrooms.

This chapter explains the rationale for connecting these two great models of learning, shows how we connected them, and lays out the brain-based principles on which their integration rests.

This chapter shows teachers how to audit and realign their curriculum so that it incorporates both learning styles and multiple intelligences, how to analyze teaching strategies to determine what styles and intelligences they engage, and how to design an instructional unit that takes advantage of both models.

This chapter introduces performance assessment, explains its relationship to learning styles and multiple intelligences, shows teachers how to use the provided assessment menus to diversify assessment, and provides guidelines for effective classroom management of the assessment process. The chapter also describes how learning styles and multiple intelligences make for a "Test Worth Taking."

This chapter explains the rationale for teaching students about styles and intelligences, and it provides methods teachers have used to teach about the two models.

List of Figures

Acknowledgments

THE QUESTION OF INFLUENCE WHEN IT COMES TO educational practice is intricate: Over the years so many teachers have informed and served as catalysts for the ideas in this book that we cannot even begin to thank them all adequately. The ideas of many teachers whose work has inspired us appear in this book, and we thank them all for their valuable contributions and their remarkable ability to put theory into high-quality practice. Among these, we would like to give special thanks to Barb Heinzman, Joanne Curran, Carl Carrozza, Charlene Larkin, Robin Cederblad, Eva Benevento, Stacey Gerhardt, Sue Ulrey, Claudia Geocaris, and Maria Ross. But we realize there have been others—many others— who have shaped our thinking and made this book possible. Though we have made every effort to contact all the teachers whose work is reflected here, some have eluded us. We wish to thank them, as well.

We would also like to thank the editorial staff at ASCD, who helped us shape our ideas and apply polish to them.

Introduction

THE CHALLENGE MANY TEACHERS FACE AFTER participating in an exciting professional development workshop is how to put good ideas into practice. Sometimes one good idea competes with another. Sometimes new ideas conflict with existing procedures.

The seed for this book was planted several years ago by Barb Heinzman, a teacher from Geneva Schools, New York, who was feeling this friction between ideas. At a workshop entitled "Teaching in the Heterogeneous Classroom," Barb approached Harvey Silver and Richard Strong, saying, "My district has conducted workshops in both learning styles and multiple intelligences. And both learning models have been really great for me and even better for my students. I can't tell you how much better student response has been since I learned how to incorporate styles and intelligences into my teaching." So far, so good, Harvey and Richard thought. Barb continued, "But I've really been wondering lately: Can you use both models at the same time? They're both so valuable, but I always find myself choosing one and having to put the other aside. It seems to me that the two models, I don't know, *need* each other somehow. There has to be a better way than having one compete with the other. What do you suggest?"

At that time, Harvey and Richard made some tentative suggestions about meeting students' needs by designing curriculum that incorporates learning styles and multiple intelligences. They noted that the hands-on aspects of the sensing-style learner often corresponded to the physical nature of the bodily-kinesthetic student. They explained that thinking-style learners frequently had high logical-mathematical intelligence and that feeling-style learners often showed strong proclivities for using their interpersonal or intrapersonal intelligences.

But as they were talking to Barb, Harvey and Richard noticed something: Most of the suggestions they were making showed the relationship between intelligences and styles, but spoke little to the question of how a teacher might use both models together to address the many ways students learn. Showing the relationships was easy. But what about the deeper connections between styles and intelligences? This bothered all of us.

Research in Motion

As a result of that conversation, we began a thorough examination of multiple-intelligence theory and learning-style models. What we wanted to know was this: How can teachers integrate these two great approaches to difference into their practice? Of course, we had many other questions, as well. Why had we unconsciously adopted an either-or approach? Is a marriage of the models into an integrated learning model possible? Do the models have discernible strengths and weaknesses? Is multiple-intelligence theory more applicable to assessment than learning styles? If so, why? Are learning styles better suited to instruction than multiple intelligences? If so, why? What can we learn from teachers? Have some teachers, through the daily use of the models in their teaching, found ways to connect learning styles and multiple intelligences? A simple conversation at a workshop led to torrents of questions.

As we reviewed lessons, curricula, teacher manuals, and instructional videos, we found that Barb Heinzman couldn't have been more correct in her feeling that the models somehow needed each other. In our research, we found many great lessons, assessment tasks, and curricula that used intelligences in exciting and inspired ways. But almost none of this intelligence-based practice related to different styles of student thought. We saw an equal amount of wonderful style-based work from classrooms across the United States. But in these lessons, assessment tasks, and curricula, we found that educators paid little attention to how the insight of multiple intelligences could be used to enrich and diversify learning. The need for integration was clearer than ever. The models were too good, their insights too valuable, to keep apart. Our driving mission became to bring these two great models of learning together in a way that would make it easy for educators to use.

What Is Integrated Learning?

Integrated learning is an approach to curriculum, instruction, and assessment designed to help teachers and schools fuse multiple intelligences and learning styles in a meaningful and practical way. It is driven by the following goals:

• *Effectiveness*, in that it maximizes the benefits and minimizes the liabilities of both learning styles and multiple intelligences.

• *Practicality*, in that it respects the demands of teachers who are being asked to meet national, state, and local standards, as well as run efficient and engaging classrooms.

• *Fairness*, in that it fosters the fullest possible range of academic diversity.

The word "integrated" implies all of these elements at once.

1. *Integrated means blended into a whole.* Two great minds of the 20th century—Howard Gardner (multiple intelligences) and Carl Jung (learning styles)—have supplied us with our two learning models. Yet, as we have found, both multiple intelligences and learning styles have particular strengths and weaknesses that directly correspond to the strengths and weaknesses of the other. This means that a truly holistic approach to education—one that allows educators to engage a full range of human diversity and meet rigorous academic standards—occurs only in the blending together of these two models.

2. *Integrated means incorporated as part of a larger picture.* From an educator's perspective, any learning theory, model, or approach is only as good as its applicability. If it cannot be used without excessive effort, it is not very valuable. The reality of schools dictates that teachers follow curriculum frameworks, meet state standards, and prepare students for state tests and academic and vocational callings. Integrated

learning respects these realities. The approach is designed so that it can be incorporated into current practices easily without asking teachers to rethink everything they do.

3. Integrated means driven by the goal of equality. We live and learn in an increasingly diverse world. New students, new issues, and new ideas appear on an almost daily basis, fueling the movement to address all forms of diversity—intellectual, physical, and cultural. By uniting the two best models we have for understanding the diverse ways students think and learn, integrated learning strives to create an environment where all learners feel that their ideas, contributions, and work are valued, and that they are able to succeed.

This book shows teachers how to use the integrated learning approach to improve curriculum, instruction, and assessment and to help students become more reflective, self-aware learners. It emphasizes the practical applications of integrated learning; and, whenever possible, it uses the work of teachers to demonstrate key ideas and points. We begin by introducing each model separately, in Chapters 1 and 2. In Chapter 3, we show how we integrated multiple intelligences and learning styles and the principles we use to guide our endeavor into integrated learning. Chapter 4 shows how teachers can use integrated learning as a tool for realigning curriculum, developing lessons, and creating instructional units. The relationship between integrated learning and performance assessment is covered in Chapter 5, with a focus on using "menus" of student products to diversify assessment practices. Finally, in Chapter 6, we show how different teachers have taught their students about both learning styles and multiple intelligences.

We hope you find this book useful, and we look forward to hearing about your experiences with integrated learning.

An Introduction to Multiple Intelligences

WHAT IS INTELLIGENCE? DEFINING INTELLIGENCE IS an endeavor that has long consumed the human mind. In ancient Greece, Plato believed that humans were largely ignorant and that the knowledge they acquired was only an insignificant abstraction of a much larger and perfect truth. In fact, Plato claimed he could only be considered smart because he was aware of his own ignorance. Humans, according to Plato, could never understand truth in its entirety; they could only begin to approach understanding through the study of geometry and logic. Aristotle, Plato's successor and student, disagreed with his teacher. In Aristotle's view, the act of gathering information was not a search after unattainable ideals but a venture of the human soul, of which the mind was an integral part. Speaking of "philosophic wisdom," Aristotle claimed that humans were capable of two great mental abilities: quickly understanding causes and situations, and making good moral choices.

The viewpoints of the ancient Greeks, of course, represent only a tiny part of the debate over what it means to be smart. Buddhist philosophy speaks of three qualities of mind—wisdom, morality, and meditation—that guide humans to correctly view, think about, and act in the world around them. Christian philosophers such as Saint Augustine and Thomas Aquinas tended to deemphasize intelligence and learning, claiming them to be secondary to faith and piety. Later, Renaissance thinkers as diverse as Niccolo Machiavelli, Leonardo Da Vinci, and Thomas More brought the human capacities of reason and creativity back to the foreground, portraying them as forces capable of controlling and even remaking the world. Since the Renaissance, nearly every philosophical and cultural movement has pondered the role of human thought and the meaning of humans' unique capacities of mind. This evolving quest stays with us today.

Despite this storied history of the concept of human intelligence, it is safe to say that no other century has seen such a shift in the definition of intelligence as we have in the 20th century. This recent evolution corresponds with our increasing understanding of the human brain and its cognitive processes. Researchers, including Reuven Feuerstein, Paul MacLean, and Roger Sperry, have revealed new insights into cognition through their work in cognitive modifiability, the triune brain, and the brain's hemispheres. Swiss psychologist Jean Piaget's theories on how humans construct knowledge have become important foundations for understanding the brain's natural learning capacities. The 20th century also saw the advent of psychometric indicators of intelligence, such as IQ testing. Yet, even as our understanding of human cognition becomes more scientific and precise, our initial question remains: What is human intelligence?

Defining Intelligence

If you were attempting to find the "essence" of intelligence by consulting a dictionary, you might get a definition like this:

> In-tel-li-gence (ĭn-tĕl-ə-jəns). The capacity to acquire and apply knowledge; the faculty of thought and reason; superior powers of mind.

But what does this mean? Is it enough? Does it tell how such capacities, faculties, and powers might manifest themselves in the people who exhibit them? Does it explain why such capacities might be considered intelligent? Does it explain how or why different cultures value intelligence? Does intelligence, according to this definition, mean the same thing for a computer programmer and a playwright? Unfortunately, this definition provides precious little practical information about intelligence. So once again, we have to ask: What is intelligence?

Perhaps one way to get the true meaning of intelligence is to consider those who use their intelligence in exceptional ways. To look at intelligence in this way, examine the list of names in Figure 1.1. How and why are the people on this list considered intelligent?

Gardner's Theory

The previous activity is similar to what Howard Gardner did when he began his work on human intelligences, and it brings us to our latest step in the evolutionary history of intelligence. With

FIGURE 1.1
FAMOUS INTELLIGENT PEOPLE

Jackie Robinson	Martin Luther King, Jr.
Maya Angelou	Billie Holliday
William Shakespeare	Marie Curie
Georgia O'Keeffe	Mahatma Gandhi
Oprah Winfrey	Carl Jung
Albert Einstein	Jim Thorpe
Louis Armstrong	Pablo Picasso
Charles Darwin	George Washington Carver

Gardner, the concept of intelligence was changed profoundly because of the way in which he expanded the parameters of intelligent behavior to include a diversity of human abilities. As he explains in "Symposium on the Theory of Multiple Intelligences" (1987):

> I performed a "thought" experiment, in which I imagined going into many different cultures and trying to identify, in each, its developed roles or "end states"—abilities highly prized in that culture, and really important for its survival. As part of the experiment, I thought about religious leaders, shamans, seers, mothers, fathers, dancers, surgeons, sculptors, hunters, businessmen, and so forth. I put myself to the challenge of coming up with a notion of cognition, that could give a better account of how the human organism can become highly competent in these very diverse kinds of capacities (pp. 79–80).

Gardner's process is different from IQ testing or other means of measuring intelligence. Rather than looking for a single, quantifiable measurement of intelligence, Gardner's method explores the way in which particular cultures value individuals and the way individuals create different products or serve their cultures in various capacities (see Figure 1.2). As he tells us:

In developing this Theory I did not start with an examination of existing tests.... I was not interested in predicting success or failure in school.... Instead, my initial intuition that there were different kinds of minds led me to sample the range of cognitive end-states as thoroughly as I could, and then to seek a model that might help us to progress in explaining how these different competences develop (Gardner, 1987, p. 80).

The Eight Intelligences

Gardner's research came to fruition in the groundbreaking *Frames of Mind* (1983), in which, by adding an "s" to "intelligence," the author broke from the tradition of IQ theory, which previously adhered to two fundamental principles:

- That human cognition was unitary.
- That individuals can adequately be described as having a single, quantifiable intelligence.

In opposition to this reductionist view of intelligence, Gardner defines intelligence as

- The ability to solve problems that one encounters in real life.
- The ability to generate new problems to solve.
- The ability to make something or offer a service that is valued within one's culture.

Gardner then divided the traditional notion of intelligence into seven distinct categories, and later (1995, 1999a) added an eighth intelligence to his model. The following paragraphs describe the eight intelligences, along with representative famous people from Figure 1.1 for each intelligence.

Verbal-Linguistic Intelligence (V) manifests itself in the ability to manipulate words for a variety of purposes: debate, persuasion, storytelling, poetry, prose writing, and instruction. People with high verbal-linguistic intelligence often love to play with words and use such devices as puns, metaphors, similes, and the like. Very often people who have strong verbal-linguistic intelligence can read for hours at a time. Their auditory skills tend to be highly

FIGURE 1.2
HOW OUR DEFINITION OF INTELLIGENCE HAS CHANGED

Old View	New View
• Intelligence was fixed	• Intelligence can be developed
• Intelligence was measured by a number	• Intelligence is not numerically quantifiable and is exhibited during a performance or problem-solving process
• Intelligence was unitary	• Intelligence can be exhibited in many ways—multiple intelligences
• Intelligence was measured in isolation	• Intelligence is measured in context/real-life situations
• Intelligence was used to sort students and predict their success	• Intelligence is used to understand human capacities and the many and varied ways students can achieve

developed, and they learn best when they can speak, listen, read, or write (*Maya Angelou, William Shakespeare*).

Logical-Mathematical Intelligence (L) is the basis for the hard sciences and all types of mathematics. People who use logical-mathematical intelligence emphasize the rational: They are usually good at finding patterns, establishing cause-and-effect relationships, conducting controlled experiments, and sequencing. Generally, they think in terms of concepts and questions and love to put ideas to the test (*Albert Einstein, Marie Curie*).

Spatial Intelligence (S) involves a high capacity for perceiving, creating, and re-creating pictures and images. Photographers, artists, engineers, architects, and sculptors all use spatial intelligence. People who are spatially intelligent are keenly perceptive of even slight visual details; can usually sketch ideas out with graphs, tables, or images; and are often able to convert words or impressions into mental images. Spatially intelligent people think in images and have a keen sense of location and direction (*Georgia O'Keeffe, Pablo Picasso*).

Musical Intelligence (M) is the ability to produce melody and rhythm, as well as to understand, appreciate, and form opinions about music. People who are able to sing in key, keep tempo, analyze musical forms, or create musical expression all exhibit musical intelligence. Musically intelligent people are sensitive to all types of nonverbal sound and the rhythms of everyday noise (*Louis Armstrong, Billie Holliday*).

Bodily-Kinesthetic Intelligence (B) is related to the physical self and the manipulation of one's own body. Those who are kinesthetically intelligent can generally handle objects or make precise bodily movements with relative ease. Their tactile sense is usually well developed, and they enjoy physical challenges and pursuits. These learners learn best by doing,

moving, and acting things out (*Jackie Robinson, Jim Thorpe*).

Interpersonal Intelligence (P) is at work in people who are naturally social. Interpersonally intelligent people work well with others and are quite sensitive to slight variations in people's moods, attitudes, and desires. Often, interpersonally intelligent people are friendly and outgoing. Most people with this intelligence know how to gauge, identify with, and react to the temperaments of others. They are generally excellent team players and managers, and they learn best when they can relate to other people (*Oprah Winfrey, Martin Luther King, Jr.*).

Intrapersonal Intelligence (I) is the ability to gain access to one's own feelings and emotional states. Intrapersonally intelligent people usually choose to work on their own, as they use and trust their self-understanding to guide them. They are in touch with their inner feelings and are able to form realistic goals and conceptions of themselves (*Mahatma Gandhi, Carl Jung*).

The eighth and most recent intelligence validated by Gardner's research is the **Naturalist Intelligence (N)**. This intelligence is found in those who are highly attuned to the natural world of plants and animals, as well as to natural geography and natural objects like rocks, clouds, and stars. People who have a high naturalist intelligence love to be outdoors and tend to notice patterns, features, and anomalies in the ecological settings they encounter. They are adept at using these patterns and features to classify and categorize natural objects and living things. Those with the naturalist intelligence show an appreciation for, and a deep understanding of, the environment (*Charles Darwin, George Washington Carver*).

It is essential to keep in mind that these intelligences are not fixed categories. To think of multiple intelligences in this way would lead to the same pigeonholing effect of IQ testing. All people, as Gardner would insist, possess all these intelligences, use all of them in different situations and contexts, and can develop each intelligence. Most people, however, demonstrate an especially high ability in one or two intelligences.

Although the effort to recognize broader, more inclusive definitions of intelligence is hardly unique to Gardner, his theory is especially powerful because he uses a rich research base that gives credence to his work. Among the wide range of fields from which Gardner culls his data are anthropology, cognitive psychology, developmental psychology, biographical studies, psychometrics, physiology, and neurology. In addition, he uses a stringent system of criteria through which a skill, talent, or mental capacity has to pass before it can be identified as true intelligence. Some of these criteria include the following:

• A unique symbol system through which the intelligence can be expressed, such as

Verbal-Linguistic—phonetic languages (English, French, Spanish)

Logical-Mathematical—numerical systems, computer languages (C+, Java)

Spatial—ideographic languages (hieroglyphics), icons (street signs, computer operating systems like Windows)

Bodily-Kinesthetic—sign language, braille, expressive dance, mime

Musical—musical notation

Interpersonal—body language

Intrapersonal—self-symbols (e.g., in dreams)

Naturalist—natural taxonomies, Linnean classification systems

• Individual histories in terms of emergence and development within an individual.
• A biological basis that is subject to change through injury to the brain.
• Expression of the intelligence in products that are culturally meaningful.

Gardner regularly notes that the eight intelligences do not necessarily represent the full scope of human capacities. In *Intelligence Reframed: Multiple Intelligences for the 21st Century* (1999b), Gardner takes a close look at four recent candidate intelligences: naturalist, spiritual, existential, and moral intelligences. In running each intelligence through his system of criteria, Gardner reaffirms naturalist as the eighth intelligence, but rejects spiritual, existential, and moral intelligences. Of the three rejected candidates, however, Gardner reserves a special place for existential intelligence, which so nearly meets the criteria that he jokingly refers to it as "intelligence $8\frac{1}{2}$."

Intelligences as Dispositions

To explore the theory of multiple intelligences (MI) more deeply, we will use critical-thinking dispositions as a lens. Critical-thinking dispositions are based on the work of Perkins, Jay, and Tishman (1993), who claim that good thinkers have certain dispositions that influence their ability to process and make sense of information. These authors recognized that critical-thinking dispositions emerged as a result of a sensitivity to certain types of behavior. As a person practices a sensitivity, the individual develops an inclination or comfort in using these types of behavior. As an inclination becomes more refined or sophisticated, the individual develops an ability and is able to apply the behavior to a variety of contexts.

The development of dispositions depends on many factors, such as the following:

• Do significant others validate this disposition?
• Are there mentors who encourage and train the individual?
• Do historical and social contexts validate this disposition?
• Does the individual receive the education needed to turn a sensitivity or inclination into a full-fledged ability?

To exemplify this point, let's look at the example of driving a car. For most Americans, driving is a way of life. Parents, relatives, and friends drive before we do, and we can usually count on these people to teach us what they know about driving when it comes time to learn this skill. From social and historical standpoints, cars are central to modern life, and knowing how to drive is highly valued in our culture. Finally, through driver education programs, we refine our developing driving skills so that our facility can become an ability. Thus, most Americans become good drivers because a social and cultural network of people, sociohistorical factors, and educational programs are in place to validate and encourage driving. In fact, this network is so firmly situated that it can be easy to forget how difficult driving is and that the skill barely existed a century ago.

Dispositional theory provides a productive means of looking at multiple intelligences. From an intelligences standpoint, a *disposition* is a sensitivity for a particular type of intelligence. A sensitivity may lead to an inclination for using that intelligence and, in the right environment and under the right circumstances, an inclination can be translated into an ability to use the intelligence in a variety of contexts. You have already seen how a skill like driving a car develops according to dispositional theory. Now let's see how each intelligence can develop in the same way. Review the information in Figure 1.3. As you view each intelligence, think about how your classroom reflects—or fails to reflect—a diversity of intelligences. This is the first step toward using multiple intelligences in your classroom. (More information on classroom applications will be provided later in this chapter and book.)

Developing Your Own Intelligence Profile

Now that you know the basics of multiple intel-

ligences, you are ready to engage in the process of self-analysis and to stimulate your own thinking about your own intelligence profile. The *Multiple Intelligences Indicator for Adults* in Appendix A is a simple, self- descriptive instrument designed to help you identify your own intelligence profile in terms of those intelligences that are your strongest and those that are your weakest. We recommend that you complete the *MI Indicator* at this point, before you proceed through the book. As you gain experience with multiple intelligences, you'll notice the particular strengths and weaknesses of your students, as well as learn to generate practical ideas to take advantage of student strengths.

Intelligence Combinations

Every person is born with eight intelligences, and all these are modifiable and teachable. Your results from the *MI Indicator* reveal your unique combination of intelligence strengths and weaknesses. Moreover, almost every complex task we encounter requires us to call forth and use several intelligences. Playing the piano requires at least three intelligences: musical, for following the music and keeping time; bodily-kinesthetic, for manipulating the fingers and feet appropriately; and spatial, for determining the relationship between keys and the sounds they produce. In addition, other intelligences, such as interpersonal for responding to facial and bodily cues from bandmates during a performance, or intrapersonal for creating personally relevant, impassioned musical expressions may be used as well.

To further illustrate this point, think about and then solve the problem in Figure 1.4 (see p. 12). There are many ways to go about solving a problem like this one. How did you do it? Think about the problem-solving process you used to solve this word problem, then complete the brief checklist in Figure 1.5 (p. 12).

FIGURE 1.3
INTELLIGENCES AS DISPOSITIONS

Disposition/Intelligence	Sensitivity to:	Inclination for:	Ability to:
Verbal-Linguistic Intelligence	the sounds, meanings, structures, and styles of language	speaking, writing, listening, reading	speak effectively (teacher, religious leader, politician) or write effectively (poet, journalist, novelist, copywriter, editor)
Logical-Mathematical Intelligence	patterns, numbers and numerical data, causes and effects, objective and quantitative reasoning	finding patterns, making calculations, forming and testing hypotheses, using the scientific method, deductive and inductive reasoning	work effectively with numbers (accountant, statistician, economist) and reason effectively (engineer, scientist, computer programmer)
Spatial Intelligence	colors, shapes, visual puzzles, symmetry, lines, images	representing ideas visually, creating mental images, noticing visual details, drawing and sketching	create visually (artist, photographer, engineer, decorator) and visualize accurately (tour guide, scout, ranger)
Bodily-Kinesthetic Intelligence	touch, movement, physical self, athleticism	activities requiring strength, speed, flexibility, hand-eye coordination, and balance	use the hands to fix or create (mechanic, surgeon, carpenter, sculptor, mason) and use the body expressively (dancer, athlete, actor)
Musical Intelligence	tone, beat, tempo, melody, pitch, sound	listening, singing, playing an instrument	create music (songwriter, composer, musician, conductor) and analyze music (music critic)
Interpersonal Intelligence	body language, moods, voice, feelings	noticing and responding to other people's feelings and personalities	work with people (administrators, managers, consultants, teachers) and help people identify and overcome problems (therapists, psychologists)
Intrapersonal Intelligence	one's own strengths, weaknesses, goals, and desires	setting goals, assessing personal abilities and liabilities, monitoring one's own thinking	meditate, reflect, exhibit self-discipline, maintain composure, and get the most out of oneself
Naturalist Intelligence	natural objects, plants, animals, naturally occurring patterns, ecological issues	identifying and classifying living things and natural objects	analyze ecological and natural situations and data (ecologists and rangers), learn from living things (zoologist, botanist, veterinarian) and work in natural settings (hunter, scout)

FIGURE 1.4
CANOE PROBLEM

Nineteen people need to cross a river. It is too rapid to swim, and there is only one canoe. Only three people can fit in the canoe at one time. One of the three must be an adult.	Only one person is an adult. How many trips across the river will be needed to get all of the children to the other side of the river?

Workspace:

FIGURE 1.5
PROBLEM-SOLVING CHECKLIST

When solving this problem, I . . .

Check	Rank		Intelligence
☐	☐	Reread the problem several times.	V
☑	☐	Visualized the problem in my head.	S
☐	☐	Drew a picture or diagram of the problem.	S
☐	☐	Used a mathematical formula to solve the problem.	L
☐	☐	Used numbers and mathematical operations.	L
☐	☐	Looked for a pattern and applied it to the solution.	L
☐	☐	Talked with someone else while working.	P
☐	☐	Sought help from someone else.	P
☐	☐	Acted out the problem.	B
☐	☐	Used concrete materials to work through the problem.	B
☑	☐	Talked to myself while working.	I
☐	☐	Thought through the problem in my head before working.	I
☐	☐	Sung or hummed to myself while working.	M
☐	☐	Thought about currents, wind, and other natural obstacles.	N
☐	☐	Chose not to do the problem.	
☐	☐	Other _____	

How does this information compare with your general profile? Did you rely on your strongest intelligence(s) to solve the problem, or did you use other less-developed intelligences in this case?

Note: V = verbal-linguistic, S = spatial, L = logical-mathematical, P = interpersonal, B = bodily-kinesthetic, I = intrapersonal, M = musical, N = naturalist intelligence.

Ways to Address and Apply Multiple Intelligences in the Classroom

Gardner's model has many implications for education. In fact, no single program or routine application of the theory can accommodate the many ways that teachers can implement multiple intelligences to help students learn and achieve in school. Good teaching strives to use multiple methods of implementing this theory. Let's look at how a few schools and teachers have used multiple intelligences to accommodate students and diversify their learning experiences.

Targeting the Development of Specific Intelligences

The inclusion of sports programs, music programs, community service clubs, debate teams, chess clubs, and art programs into school curricula all speak to intelligence targeting. In classroom settings, teachers often target specific intelligences through activity centers (Armstrong, 1994) by setting up stations throughout the classroom with learning tools relating to each intelligence. For instance, a verbal-linguistic learning center might include books and word processors, whereas a bodily-kinesthetic center would include manipulatives and hands-on items. These centers may last the whole year or only a few days or weeks, depending on the instructional goals of the teacher. Further, activity centers may be "open-ended," giving students freedom to choose their own endeavors, or they may be topic-specific by providing an activity that relates specifically to instructional objectives. For example, at the spatial center you might ask students to create a comic strip that shows how Shirley Temple Wong adjusted to life in America in the book *In The Year of the Boar and Jackie Robinson*.

Differentiating Instruction Through Use of All the Intelligences

Because Gardner tells us we all possess and can develop each intelligence, many teachers strive to provide instruction that is rich and regimented in its use of multiple intelligences. The lesson in Figure 1.6 represents the work of Charlene Larkin, of Whitney Point Central, New York. Notice how each instructional episode in her lesson is linked to the intelligences it will ask students to deploy. By keeping track of the intelligences activated in each lesson, Charlene ensures students are given the chance to work in all the intelligences, including their weakest and strongest.

Diversifying Curriculum So That It Is Intelligence-Rich and Intelligence-Fair

Sometimes a map, like the "curriculum wheel" in Figure 1.7 (p. 17), can broadly integrate multiple intelligences into a curriculum; this spatial representation can help us see how a curriculum or unit can be designed around intelligences. Such a map can serve as a brainstorming tool: Teachers can consider a tapestry of curricular options and ideas. Teachers can expand and refine options that fit well with the curriculum, and they can discard those options that feel forced or interfere with lesson objectives.

Providing Students with Choices of Activities and Assessments

Wendy Ecklund Lambert (1997), a high school history teacher in Orlando, Florida, uses a project-planning form to give her students leverage in choosing formats for a research project on the Expansion Era in American history. She provides students with a list of 65 topics and allows them to choose the format for their final presentation. Her students create skits, watercolor paintings, telegraphs, board games, eulogies, historical lectures, storybooks, puppet shows, advertisements, and other demonstrations

FIGURE 1.6
SAMPLE INSTRUCTIONAL UNIT

To what extent does the activity address the particular style and type of intelligence?

Key: XXX = to a great extent
XX = considerable
X = somewhat

Intelligences:
V = Verbal-Linguistic, **S** = Spatial, **L** = Logical-Mathematical, **P** = Interpersonal,
B = Bodily-Kinesthetic, **I** = Intrapersonal, **M** = Musical, **N** = Naturalist.

Activity	Intelligence			
Sharing: Each student brings to class his or her favorite teddy bear. The students sit in a circle and introduce their teddy bears to the class. (Tell his name and what makes him special.)	V	X X	B	X X
	L		P	X X
	S		I	X
	M		N	
Graphing: The teacher makes a bar graph on the floor, and the students place their teddy bears on the floor according to the characteristics (e.g., brown bears). The students can count the number of bears and then make a sentence that describes the data.	V	X X	B	X X
	L	X	P	
	S	X X	I	
	M		N	
Grouping/Organizing: Students are asked to figure out the different ways they can design a teddy bear by grouping their bears according to common characteristics.	V	X	B	X
	L	XXX	P	
	S	X	I	
	M		N	

FIGURE 1.6—*continued*
SAMPLE INSTRUCTIONAL UNIT

Activity	Intelligence			
Designing: Students design a teddy bear after reading a teddy bear order form that identifies the type of fur, color, clothes, and expressions that have been selected.	V	X	B	XXX
	L	X X	P	
	S	X X	I	
	M		N	

Fur

curly

long

short

Color

black

brown

other

Face

smile

frown

surprised

Clothes

shirt or dress

pants

hat

Source: Charlene Larkin, Whitney Point Central School, New York.

FIGURE 1.7
CURRICULUM WHEEL

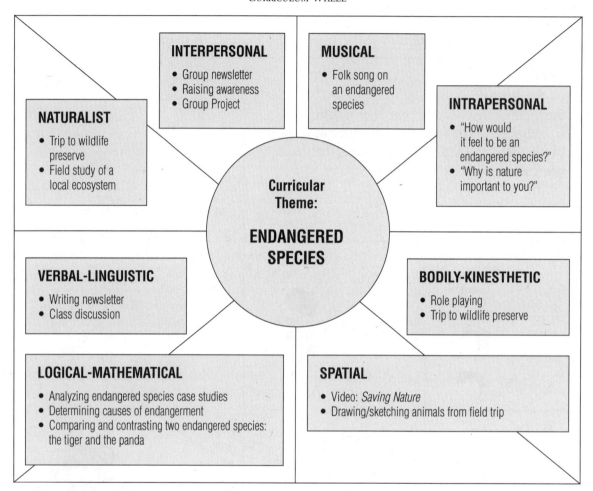

of their learning using various intelligences. She reports, "As students learn from their own projects and those of their classmates, they gain important insights about themselves and their abilities" (p. 53).

In a middle school earth science classroom in Clayton County, Georgia, a similar choice format allowed students to demonstrate their understanding of sedimentary, igneous, and metamorphic rocks, yielding a marvelous variety of products. One group of students chose to create written narratives (verbal-linguistic intelligence), another drew diagrams (spatial), and a third chose to physically represent each rock type (bodily-kinesthetic). The bodily-kinesthetic students lay on top of each other to show sedimentary layers, formed a pyramid and used their hands to simulate an eruption of igneous rock, and tangled their arms and hands together to show the interconnectedness of metamorphic rock.

Supporting Student Learning in a Particular Intelligence by Allowing

Students to Use Another More-Developed Intelligence to Enhance Their Understanding of Content

Often, in completing tasks or engaging in activities, we will rely on our strongest intelligences to make sense of material. This reliance on the most-developed intelligences is known as "translation." For example, have you ever been thoroughly confused by a set of written directions, but known exactly how to get to a destination after looking at a map of the same directions? Or maybe for you it's the opposite—written directions pose no problem whereas the overlapping strands of roadways seem impossibly complicated. Clearly, what works for one person might not for another because of individuals' different intelligence profiles. By allowing students to process information according to the intelligence they use best, you provide a scaffolding for students, helping them gain mastery over essential content.

For instance, many teachers use a strategy known as "Visualizing Vocabulary" (Silver, Strong, & Commander, 1998) to tap into the power of translation. The strategy is based on the fact that a student who is stronger in spatial intelligence than verbal-linguistic can learn vocabulary words more effectively by using pictures to associate with the correctly spelled words. The student begins by defining the word. Then the student finds three to four pictures or draws an original picture that illustrates the definition. Finally, the student must explain why the pictures are good examples of the word. This strategy allows students to learn how to use their strongest intelligence to support their learning in a weaker intelligence. Figures 1.8–1.10 show other examples of how teachers help students translate content through more-developed intelligences.

Intelligences as Pathways to Understanding Broad Topics

A final method for incorporating intelligences into teaching comes from Howard Gardner's recent book, *The Disciplined Mind: What All Students Should Understand* (1999a). In this book, Gardner argues that curriculum should be designed around topics or phenomena that he calls "icebergs"—topics like evolution, the music of Mozart, and the Holocaust, which are inexhaustibly rich sources of learning. In fashioning

FIGURE 1.8
EXAMPLE OF TRANSLATION 1

Musical Intelligence in Elementary Language Arts

Nouns and verbs are really cool
Use them correctly,
Don't sound like a fool.
Nouns show people, places, things.
Verbs show action and state of being.

FIGURE 1.9
EXAMPLE OF TRANSLATION 2

Verbal-Linguistic Intelligence in Middle School Biology

Cinquain

Bacteria
microscopic, organism,
helping, harming, invading
needed to sustain life
germs

FIGURE 1.10
EXAMPLE OF TRANSLATION 3

**Logical-Mathematical Intelligence in Secondary American History:
Statement-Evidence Organizer**

Directions: Preview these statements before the lecture. Decide whether you agree or disagree with each statement. Afterwards, use your notes to collect evidence that supports or refutes each statement.

Evidence For	Statement	Evidence Against
	Lincoln was a self-made man.	
	Lincoln cared more about preserving the Union than about slaves' rights.	
	If it weren't for Lincoln, American history would have been radically different.	
	Lincoln had to make the hardest decisions of any U.S. President before him.	

a curriculum around these broad and robust topics, teachers and students should be engaged in developing a deep understanding of the universal concepts of truth, beauty, and goodness as they relate to the topic. Multiple intelligences, in this approach, become tools or pathways for helping students enter into the topic, explore its complexities, and demonstrate their evolving understanding of its central concepts.

Whereas Gardner seems to be provoking us to think of these explorations as year-long, or at least half-year-long endeavors, Figure 1.11 shows what his notion of intelligence-based exploration of a broad, rich topic might look like in a more traditional, two- to three-week, 4th grade curriculum unit on slavery.

Analyzing the Types of Intelligences Used in Your Classroom

Each intelligence represents a door to understanding the diversity in your classroom. Each intelligence can also serve as a unique and exciting way of focusing on the content students need to learn. Review the dispositions chart in Figure 1.3 (p. 11), which shows how

FIGURE 1.11
4TH GRADE SLAVERY UNIT

	Verbal-Linguistic	Logical Mathematical
Entryways into Topic	Read aloud *Nettie's Trip South* by Ann Warren Turner, which describes a New England girl's trip into the Deep South and her encounter with slavery. Students analyze text and pictures to form hypotheses about why slavery happened.	Students study slavery statistics: where slaves came from, plantation expenses and profits, number of deaths, number of runaways, etc. They use this information to develop a list of questions about slavery they want to answer.
	Interpersonal and Verbal-Linguistic	**Spatial**
Exploration and Research	Students read excerpts from Virginia Hamilton's *People Who Could Fly* and *Many Thousands Gone*, which uses memoirs, diaries, and documents to tell the story of slavery. The goal is to help students understand slaves' experiences, values, and literature in a more personal way.	Students examine plantation maps, trying to understand how slavery created different lives for masters and slaves, as well as how the system worked.
	Intrapersonal	**Musical and Interpersonal**
Assessment (Demonstrating Understanding)	Students create a diary of a slave living in Washington, D.C., who heard the arguments for and against slavery in Congress, and was eventually freed by the Emancipation Proclamation.	Students study African American spirituals and, in groups, write and perform a play with both words and music about "Jubilee Day." Students must explore the hopes and fears of both slaves and masters on the day slavery ended.

each intelligence develops into an ability. Then examine Figure 1.12, which describes classroom activities and applications for each intelligence. Collect examples from your own teaching that use each of these intelligences. Then identify the most-represented and least-represented intelligences in your classroom:

What do you need to do to create an intelligence-balanced classroom?

FIGURE 1.12
COLLECTING CLASSROOM EXAMPLES

Intelligence	Examples of Classroom Activities	Examples from My Classroom
Verbal-Linguistic	discussions, debates, journal writing, conferences, essays, stories, poems, storytelling, listening activities, reading	
Logical-Mathematical	calculations, experiments, comparisons, number games, using evidence, formulating and testing hypotheses, deductive and inductive reasoning	
Spatial	concept maps, graphs, charts, art projects, metaphorical thinking, visualization, videos, slides, visual presentations	
Bodily-Kinesthetic	role-playing, dance, athletic activities, manipulatives, hands-on demonstrations, concept miming	
Musical	playing music, singing, rapping, whistling, clapping, analyzing sounds and music	
Interpersonal	community-involvement projects, discussions, cooperative learning, team games, peer tutoring, conferences, social activities, sharing	
Intrapersonal	student choice, journal writing, self-evaluation, personal instruction, independent study, discussing feelings, reflecting	
Naturalist	ecological field trips, environmental study, caring for plants and animals, outdoor work, pattern recognition	

An Introduction to Learning Styles

THE CONCEPT OF QUATERNITY OR "FOURNESS" AS A way of thinking about human differences has a long-standing place in history. From the ancient Greeks all the way to the Renaissance, the prevailing concept of human personality was that of Hippocrates's humors. Hippocrates was a Greek physician who claimed that all people had four liquids or humors in the body—blood, black bile, phlegm, and yellow bile. Ideally the amount of each humor was to be roughly equal, resulting in a properly balanced human. However, an excess of any of the four humors would develop into one of the four types of personalities: melancholic, sanguine, choleric, and phlegmatic. In the late 1700s, English poet and artist William Blake wrote of the four Zoas or life energies that animated human existence. Blake called these Zoas Tharmas (the body and its senses), Luvah (the heart and its capacity for love), Urizen (the head and its ability to reason), and Urthona (the spirit and its potential for creative imagination). Elsewhere, in the spiritual stories of the North American Plains Indians, the sacred Medicine Wheel tells of four human personality traits—wisdom, clarity of perception, introspection, and understanding one's emotions—and links them to the animal world.

More recently, Swiss psychologist Carl Jung (1923) reconceptualized human fourness as *psychological types* or different kinds of personalities humans can exhibit. In Jung's paradigm, human difference is based on two fundamental cognitive functions: *perception* (how we absorb information), and *judgment* (how we process the absorbed information). We can perceive or absorb information in two ways, either concretely through sensing or abstractly through intuition. We can judge or process information in two ways as well, either through the logic of thinking or the subjectivity of feeling.

As Jung explains these four dimensions of personality, each corresponds "to the obvious means by which consciousness obtains its orientation to experience: sensation [**sensing**] tells you that something exists; **thinking** tells you what it is; **feeling** tells you whether it is agreeable or not; and **intuition** tells you from whence it comes and where it is going" (1923, p. 481). In addition, Jung also considered how active or reflective an individual is while interacting (introversion versus extroversion). At the center of his model, however, lies a familiar quaternity symbolized by Jung as a mandala in which each function represents a universal characteristic of human personality (see Figure 2.1).

FIGURE 2.1
FUNCTION MANDALA

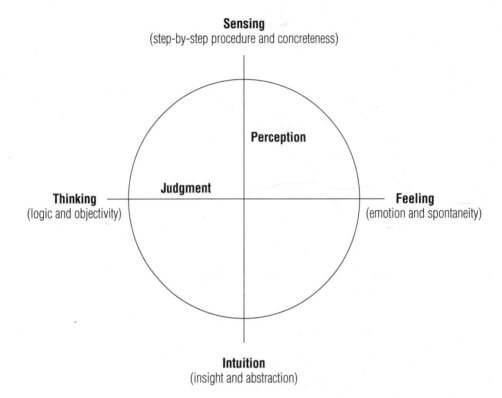

An Overview of Perceptions and Judgments

Perception: Sensing and Intuition

We all perceive the world in which we live. We achieve this perception in two ways: through sensing and through intuition. Sensing is a concrete function that employs the five senses—hearing, sight, taste, smell, and touch—to gather information. Through sensing we take in the facts and details of the world around us, and we process the characteristics of the people, places, and things that make this world up—characteristics such as crunchy, red, round, and sweet. Intuition, on the other hand, is a more abstract function that helps the mind understand what

might be by using guesswork, inspiration, and insight to find the patterns, generalizations, and meanings behind the facts and details. Without intuition we would be unable to see the big picture, to understand that so many individual trees make up a forest, to treat an object that is crunchy, red, round, and sweet as an apple.

We all rely on both of these functions. We need *sensing* to characterize and clarify reality, and we need *intuition* to determine the big concepts that give reality meaning and to predict potential changes within that reality. But we all rely on each function to differing degrees. Those who base their perceptions mainly on sensing like to live and work in the here and now. They are motivated by practicality and usefulness,

22

they generally have a realistic outlook on life, and they like to operate according to procedures and toward definite goals. When their purpose becomes unclear or when the details become complicated, sensors often get frustrated. Sensors like results and value the hard work it takes to achieve them. Intuitives, on the other hand, like flexibility and the freedom to explore possibilities and ideas. They trust their own insights, go where their inspiration and vision take them, and often feel constrained by procedures. Unlike the sensor, who prefers to keep things separate, the intuitive sees little value in the maxim, "Never mix business with pleasure." (See Figure 2.2.)

FIGURE 2.2
SELF-ASSESSMENT (PERCEPTION)

Take a moment to reflect on your own perception preferences. Are you more focused on the facts and details of sensing or the big picture and patterns of intuition? Place an X on the line below to indicate where you fall on the sensing-intuition axis:

Sensing _____ Intuition

Judgment: Thinking and Feeling

Perception is only half of the story. Once information is perceived through sensing and intuition, the mind needs to make a judgment about how to use it. The mind can do this in two ways: through thinking and through feeling. Objectivity is the hallmark of the thinking function. Through thinking we establish distance from a situation and employ logic, reason, and evidence to analyze it. Thinking allows us to see the connective logic that ties causes to effects and action to consequences. The other judgment function, feeling, works on the subjective rather than the objective, allowing the individual to develop a personal perspective. Rather than seeking the logical connections, feelers look for the human connections that make life rich and meaningful. Through feeling we react, develop our personal values, and forge emotional relationships with the people around us.

As with the perception functions, all of us use both judgment functions. Thinking keeps our decisions rational, while feeling gives us purpose for making decisions. However, most of us tend to rely more heavily on one function than the other. Those who rely mostly on thinking are guided by standards of logic, organization, order, and objectivity when making decisions. Thinkers do not require social approval for their decisions and are often uncomfortable with emotional situations. From the thinker's perspective, everything can be treated rationally. Feelers disagree with the idea that everything succumbs to the laws of reason. They make decisions less with their heads and more with their hearts. Subjectivity, or how things feel, rather than objectivity, or how things can be analyzed, is the feeler's guiding principle for making decisions. Feelers are spontaneous and social people who like to bounce their ideas off others and who look for approval from their peers. To the feeler, everything is personal. (See Figure 2.3.)

FIGURE 2.3
SELF-ASSESSMENT (JUDGMENT)

What is your preference when it comes to thinking and feeling? When you make a decision, do you rely more on logic and objectivity (thinking) or do you go on how the situation feels to you (feeling)? Place an X on the line below to show your preference:

Thinking _____ Feeling

The wisdom in Jung's work can be observed in famous teams whose members each exemplify a particular function. In the television show *Star Trek*, for example, we see the hard logic of Spock (thinking), the free-wheeling and speculative Captain Kirk (intuition), the hands-on engineer Scotty (sensing), and the caring Dr. Bones (feeling). The characters in the sitcom *Seinfeld* also represent the four functions, recast as humorous dysfunctions: Jerry's obsession with analyzing everything (thinking), Kramer's off-the-wall plans and ideas (intuition), George's procedural rigidity (sensing), and Elaine's burning need to be loved and appreciated (feeling).

Out of Jung's model of psychological type came a maelstrom of activity and research on human personality. Central to this movement was Isabel Myers (1962), who developed the most famous application of Jung's model—the Myers-Briggs Type Indicator (MBTI)—used to identify an individual's personality type. Recent estimates show that some 3 million Americans take the MBTI each year (Briggs-Myers, 1993).

If Jung developed the model of personality type and Myers applied it, then a new generation of researchers can be said to have worked through its implications and discovered how it can be successfully applied to education. Key researchers of this generation include: Bernice McCarthy (1982), Kathleen Butler (1984), Anthony Gregorc (1985), Harvey Silver and J. Robert Hanson (1998), and Carolyn Mamchur (1996). Although all these learning-styles theorists interpret human personality in a variety of ways, all of their work is marked by a similar focus on the *process* of learning. Unlike multiple intelligences, a model concerned primarily with the content or the "what" of learning, styles focus on the "how" of learning. Through learning styles, we can talk about the way individuals learn and how their preferences for certain types of thinking processes affect their learning behaviors.

From Function to Style

Using the Silver and Hanson (1998) design as our basis, let's explore how the four basic functions combine to form a process-oriented learning-style model. Starting again with intersecting functions, we see how each quadrant is composed of a perception preference (sensing or intuition) and a judgment preference (thinking or feeling), yielding four possible combinations, as Figure 2.4 shows.

Sensing-Thinking Learners, or Mastery Learners (ST)

Capsule Description. *Realistic, practical, and matter-of-fact.* Sensing Thinkers are efficient and results-oriented, preferring action to words, and involvement to theory. They have a high energy level for doing things that are pragmatic, logical, and useful.

Approach to Learning. Sensing-Thinking learners like to complete their work in an organized and efficient manner. They tend to prefer hands-on and technical learning, and focus more on things than ideas or people. They have an appetite for work, need to be kept busy, and require immediate feedback. They would rather do almost anything than remain in their seat listening to someone speak. They need to be active, to be doing, to see tangible results from their efforts, and to be in control of the task.

ST learners ask "What?" and "How?" They prefer step-by-step directions when assigned a task and become impatient if the instructions become long and involved. More than any other learner, they want to know exactly what is expected of them. They need to know what they have to do, how they are to do it, and when it is to be done. ST learners will often lose interest in an activity if it moves too slowly, or if they can see no practical use for it.

FIGURE 2.4
THE FOUR LEARNING STYLES

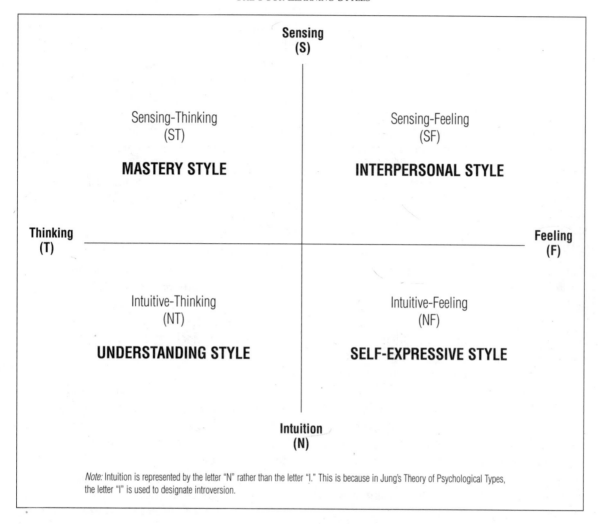

Sensing
(S)

Sensing-Thinking
(ST)

MASTERY STYLE

Sensing-Feeling
(SF)

INTERPERSONAL STYLE

Thinking
(T)

Feeling
(F)

Intuitive-Thinking
(NT)

UNDERSTANDING STYLE

Intuitive-Feeling
(NF)

SELF-EXPRESSIVE STYLE

Intuition
(N)

Note: Intuition is represented by the letter "N" rather than the letter "I." This is because in Jung's Theory of Psychological Types, the letter "I" is used to designate introversion.

Sensing-Thinking learners need clearly structured environments focusing on factual mastery of skills, and an opportunity to apply them to something practical or to demonstrate proficiency in the skill. They prefer assignments that have right or wrong responses rather than open-ended or interpretive ones. ST learners are highly motivated by competition, learning games, grades, gold stars, and are called Mastery Learners because they seek to master skills and content.

Intuitive-Thinking Learners, or Understanding Learners (NT)

Capsule Description. *Theoretical, intellectual, and knowledge-oriented.* Intuitive Thinkers prefer to be challenged intellectually and to think things through for themselves. They are curious about ideas, have a tolerance for theory, a taste for complex problems, and a concern for long-range consequences.

Approach to Learning. Intuitive-Thinking learners approach learning in a logical, organized, systematic fashion, bringing organization and structure to people and things. They take time to plan, organize ideas, and determine necessary resources before beginning work on an assignment.

NTs prefer to work independently or with other thinking types and require little feedback until their work is completed. They do not like to be pressed for time. When working on something of interest, time is meaningless. They display a great deal of patience and persistence in completing difficult assignments if the assignment has captured their interest.

NT learners attack problems by breaking them down into their component parts. They like to reason things out and to look for logical relationships. Their thought processes follow a cause-and-effect line of reasoning. They are constantly asking "why?" and their questions tend to be provocative. Their concern is for relevance and meaning.

Intuitive Thinkers are avid readers. Their learning is vicarious; therefore, abstract symbols, formulae, the written word, and technical illustrations are preferred sources for collecting data. NTs usually display a facility for language and express their ideas in detail. Everything they touch turns into words, spoken or written. They enjoy arguing a point based on logical analysis. In discussion, they often play the role of "devil's advocate" or purposefully argue an opposite point of view.

Intuitive Thinkers are concerned with objective truth more than fact. For them, everything needs to be logical and supported, and they are often upset by mistakes or gaps in logic. Intuitive thinkers are called Understanding Learners because they probe ideas deeply and thoroughly to come to an understanding.

Intuitive-Feeling Learners, or Self-Expressive Learners (NF)

Capsule Description. *Curious, insightful, and imaginative.* Intuitive Feelers are the ones who dare to dream, are committed to their values, are open to alternatives, and are constantly searching for new and unusual ways to express themselves.

Approach to Learning. Intuitive-Feeling students approach learning eager to explore ideas, generate new solutions to problems, and discuss moral dilemmas. Their interests are varied and unpredictable, but they prefer activities that allow them to use their imaginations and do things in unique ways. They are turned off by routine or rote assignments and prefer questions that are open ended, such as "What would happen if . . . ?"

NFs are highly motivated by their own interests. Things of interest will be done inventively and well. Things that they do not like may be done poorly or forgotten altogether. When engaged in a project that intrigues them, time is meaningless. Intuitive Feelers operate by an "internal clock" and therefore often feel constrained or frustrated by external rules or schedules.

Intuitive Feelers are independent and non-conforming. They do not fear being different and are usually aware of their own and others' impulses. They are open to the irrational and not confined by convention. They are sensitive to beauty and symmetry and will comment on the aesthetic characteristics of things.

NFs prefer not to follow step-by-step procedures but rather to move where their intuitions take them. They prefer to find their own solutions, rather than being told what to do or how to do it. They are able to take intuitive leaps, and they trust their own insights. Intuitive Feelers often take circuitous routes to solving problems and may not be able to explain how they arrived at the answer.

Highly adaptable to new situations, Intuitive Feelers are flexible in thought and action. They prefer dynamic environments with many resources and materials. Intuitive Feelers, more than any other type, are less likely to be disturbed by changes in routine. They are comfortable working with a minimum of directions. Their work is sometimes scattered and may look chaotic to STs and NTs. Intuitive-Feeling learners are often engaged in a number of activities at the same time, and move from one to the other according to where their interests take them. Often, they start more projects than they can finish. Intuitive-Feelers are called Self-Expressive learners because they look for unique and creative ways to express themselves.

Sensing-Feeling Learners or Interpersonal Learners (SF)

Capsule Description. *Sociable, friendly, and interpersonally oriented.* Sensing-Feeling learners are sensitive to people's feelings—their own and others'. They prefer to learn about things that directly affect people's lives, rather than impersonal facts or theories.

Approach to Learning. Sensing Feelers take a personal approach to learning. They work best when emotionally involved in what they are being asked to learn. SF learners tend to be spontaneous and often act on impulse or what "feels right." They are interested in people and like to listen to and talk about people and their feelings. They like to be helpful to others and need to be recognized for their efforts.

SF learners, particularly, enjoy personal attention. They need to feel relaxed, comfortable, and to enjoy themselves while they learn. They like to think out loud, to work with other students, to share their ideas, and to get the reactions of their friends. They much prefer cooperation to competition, and they need reassurance or praise that lets them know they are doing well. They are greatly influenced by the likes and dislikes of others. They may complete a task as a means of pleasing someone rather than because they are interested in the task itself.

The question that the SF seeks to answer is, "Of what value is this to me?" SF learners look for connections between what they are learning and their personal experiences. They are motivated by opportunities to express values, feelings, and personal memories. For SF learners, there is little distinction between school and life; and when school becomes far removed from human content and real-life issues, they may become bored or disengaged, or they may talk to a classmate.

As with multiple intelligences, we must avoid making the mistake of using styles to make simple categories into which students fit. Everyone uses all four styles throughout life, depending on the situation and context (see Figure 2.5).

Styles as Dispositions

As with multiple intelligences, styles can be looked at more deeply by linking them to Perkins, Jay, and Tishman's (1993) critical thinking dispositions. In the case of learning styles, a disposition begins as a sensitivity to certain types of input that can become an inclination for a certain type of behavior and, finally, can be refined so that the individual develops an ability to apply the behavior in diverse and meaningful ways. Figure 2.6 (see p. 29) shows how styles as dispositions play out.

Developing Your Own Style Profile

Now that you understand the basics of learning styles, you can engage in the process of self-analysis and begin thinking more carefully about your personal learning-style profile, using the provided portions of the *Learning Styles Inventory for Adults* (see Appendix B). Follow the directions on the instrument to develop your profile. It would be helpful to do this before you continue reading.

FIGURE 2.5
STYLE SUMMARY

The Sensing-Thinking (ST) or Mastery Learner	The Sensing-Feeling (SF) or Interpersonal Learner
PREFERS TO LEARN BY: • seeing tangible results • practicing what he has learned • following directions one step at a time • being active rather than passive • knowing exactly what is expected of her, how well the task must be done and why **LEARNS BEST FROM:** • drill • demonstration • practice • hands-on experience **LIKES:** • doing things that have immediate, practical use • being acknowledged for thoroughness and detail • praise for prompt and complete work • immediate feedback (rewards, privileges, etc.) **DISLIKES:** • completing tasks for which there are no practical uses • activities that require imagination and intuition • activities with complex directions • open-ended activities without closure or pay-off • activities that focus on feelings or other intangible results	**PREFERS TO LEARN BY:** • studying about things that directly affect people's lives rather than impersonal facts or theories • receiving personal attention and encouragement from his teachers • being part of a team—collaborating with other students • activities that help her learn about herself and how she feels about things **LEARNS BEST FROM:** • group experiences and projects • loving attention • personal expression and personal encounters • role playing **LIKES:** • receiving personal attention and encouragement • opportunities to be helpful in class • personal feedback • sharing personal feelings and experiences with others **DISLIKES:** • long periods of working alone silently • emphasis on factual detail • highly competitive games where someone loses • detailed and demanding routines
The Intuitive-Thinking (NT) or Understanding Learner	The Intuitive-Feeling (NF) or Self- Expressive Learner
PREFERS TO LEARN BY: • studying about ideas and how things are related • planning and carrying out a project of his own making and interest • arguing or debating a point based on logical analysis • problem solving that requires collecting, organizing, and evaluating data **LEARNS BEST FROM:** • lectures • reading • logical discussions and debates • projects of personal interest **LIKES:** • time to plan and organize her work • working independently or with other intuitive-thinking types • working with ideas and things that challenge him to think, to explore, to master **DISLIKES:** • routine or rote assignments • memorization • concern for details • rigid rules and predetermined procedures	**PREFERS TO LEARN BY:** • being creative and using his imagination • planning and organizing her work in her own creative ways • working on a number of things at one time • searching for alternative solutions to problems beyond those normally considered • discussing real problems and looking for real solutions **LEARNS BEST FROM:** • creative and artistic activities • open-ended discussions of personal and social values • activities that enlighten and enhance—myths, human achievement, dramas, etc. **LIKES:** • contemplation • being able to learn through discovery • opportunity to plan and pursue his own interests • recognition for personal insights and discoveries **DISLIKES:** • too much attention to detail • facts, memorization, rote learning • tasks with predetermined correct answers • detailed and demanding routines

FIGURE 2.6
STYLES AS DISPOSITIONS

Disposition/ Style	Sensitivity to:	Inclination for:	Ability to:
Sensing-Thinking MASTERY	acts details physical actions steps	remembering describing manipulating ordering	organize report build plan and carry out projects
Intuitive-Thinking UNDERSTANDING	gaps/flaws questions patterns ideas	analyzing testing/proving examining connecting	argue research develop theories explain
Intuitive-Feeling SELF-EXPRESSIVE	hunches images possibilities inspiration	predicting/speculating imagining generating ideas developing insights	develop original solutions think metaphorically articulate ideas express and create
Sensing-Feeling INTERPERSONAL	feelings people gut reactions experiences	supporting personalizing expressing emotions learning from experience	build trust and rapport empathize respond teach

The Learning-Style Profile

Every person develops and uses a mixture of learning styles throughout life, usually flexing and adapting styles to fit various contexts and to meet a variety of learning demands. Yet, as your learning-style profile may have shown, most people favor one or two styles over the others. In this regard, styles can be compared to muscles: The more they are used and stretched, the more developed and powerful they become, whereas those that are used only minimally will not develop fully. Also, like muscles, styles can always be strengthened through practice.

Aside from the personal profile, which reflects a general set of preferences and strengths, specific tasks also engage a variety of learning styles. The simple act of reading, for example, requires us to draw on all four styles to reveal the multiple layers on which a text operates. For example, read the excerpt in Figure 2.7 (p. 30). As you read, try to "hear yourself thinking."

To read a passage like Abraham Lincoln's "Gettysburg Address" deeply, we must interact with it and perform multiple operations on it so that its meanings and nuances are apparent to us. Figure 2.8 (p. 31) explores the relationship of these operations to style.

How do the results of this activity correlate with the learning-style profile you developed previously? Did you use all four learning styles? Did you rely only on your strongest style(s)?

FIGURE 2.7
THE GETTYSBURG ADDRESS

Four score and seven years ago our fathers brought forth on this continent, a new nation, conceived in Liberty, and dedicated to the proposition that all men are created equal.

Now we are engaged in a great civil war, testing whether that nation, or any nation so conceived and so dedicated, can long endure. We are met on a great battlefield of that war. We have come to dedicate a portion of that field, as a final resting place for those who here gave their lives that that nation might live. It is altogether fitting and proper that we should do this.

But, in a larger sense, we can not dedicate—we can not consecrate—we can not hallow—this ground. The brave men, living and dead, who struggled here, have consecrated it, far above our poor power to add or detract. The world will little note, nor long remember what we say here, but it can never forget what they did here. It is for us the living, rather, to be dedicated here to the unfinished work which they who fought here have thus far so nobly advanced. It is rather for us to be here dedicated to the great task remaining before us—that from these honored dead we take increased devotion to that cause for which they gave the last full measure of devotion—that we here highly resolve that these dead shall not have died in vain—that this nation, under God, shall have a new birth of freedom—and that government of the people, by the people, for the people, shall not perish from the earth.

Abraham Lincoln
November 19, 1863

Ways to Address and Apply Learning Styles in the Classroom

Good thinkers know that information must be looked at in various ways. By locking ourselves into one way of thinking, we become rigid and unable to adapt to different situations and ideas. For this reason, educators should help students develop their unique learning-style profile, define individual strengths and weaknesses, and give advice on how to balance the entire picture.

There are, as you might imagine, dozens of ways to incorporate learning styles into teaching. Here are five excellent starting points: helping students develop specific styles, differentiating instruction, integrating curriculum, providing choices to students, and supporting students' choice of styles.

Targeting the Development of Specific Styles

Many teachers choose to focus on particular styles over the course of the year, depending

FIGURE 2.8
READING AND STYLE

Which of the following mental activities did you perform during reading?

- At the Mastery (ST) level, we must determine the gist or basic, literal meaning of the text.

- At the Understanding (NT) level, we find themes and patterns, and we develop an interpretation of the reading, seeking out textual evidence that confirms or challenges our interpretation.

- At the Self-Expressive (NF) level, we seek to bring the passage to life by looking for and developing images to make our reading resonant, as well as by paying attention to the aesthetics of the piece.

- At the Interpersonal Level (SF) we look for connections the reading makes with our personal experiences, feelings, and prior knowledge. Often we seek others with whom we can discuss our ideas.

---

on the class's needs. Following are the stories of four teachers who are concentrating on the development of specific styles with their students:

NT

Inquiry is at the heart of Mary Daley's 1st-grade classroom in Parsippany, New Jersey. In her words, "My students are at an age where they are really excited about discovering the world around them—they have tons of questions, which I use to frame their learning." When they started a unit about ocean life, the class began by brainstorming all of the questions about this unit and recording their questions on the board—Why is seawater salty? How do fish breathe under water? and so on. Then Mary and her students chose books to read together to

research their questions. After their reading, they were able to answer some of their questions, but they also found they had even more questions to ask. Again, the class first recorded the questions they generated and then conducted research using books from the library and asking questions of their parents, siblings, and other teachers and students around the school. Mary thrives on her students' curiosity, and her students benefit from being so actively engaged in directing their own learning process.

ST

Theodora Lacey of Teaneck, New Jersey, finds that her 8th graders can be overwhelmed by the amount of material her Life Science class covers and finds Direct Instruction can make the information more manageable for students. She says, "I try to show my students how to organize their learning so they can manage it, recall it, and apply it." Starting in September, Theodora uses an overhead projector to work through difficult passages from the textbook with students. In the beginning of the year, she models how to use questions to pick out relevant information and create usable notes, allowing students to practice using the technique in groups and independently as they read later sections. Over the next two months, she continues this process to teach students how to use a variety of techniques—concept mapping, visualizations, two-column notes, main idea notes—and how to select the most appropriate technique in different situations. By the end of November, students have made tremendous gains in their abilities to study effectively, process complex ideas, internalize essential concepts, and make connections between old and new learning.

NF

Sherry Gibbon, a high school history teacher in Penn Yan, New York, says, "The more experience students have in working with metaphors, the better their thinking and writing become. I love when they begin to use metaphors in their own writing and discussion." To help her students develop this powerful method of communication, Sherry asks her students to think of historical periods as recipes. For instance, during their examination of the Progressive Era, the class studies a variety of recipes and discusses how different ingredients react (e.g., yeast causes dough to rise, warm milk activates yeast, cinnamon adds spice and flavor). Working in small groups, students are challenged to determine the "ingredients" or forces at work during the Progressive Era in American history and to formulate the effects and reactions of each of their chosen ingredients. Sometimes, students have "Bake-Off" competitions in which recipes are judged by teachers and other students on the basis of content, clarity, creativity, and presentation skills.

SF

As part of their school's community-based learning project, 5th graders in Dade County, Florida, identified a community problem: lost pets. In response, students decided to publish and distribute informational pamphlets for the community. Students went to the local library to study other types of informational pamphlets and, with the help of their teacher, developed guidelines for the length, style, visual appeal, and structure of their pamphlets. They interviewed local veterinarians and volunteers at their community's animal shelter to find out why pets run away, what can be done to prevent it, and how to locate a lost pet. Working in groups, students used what they had learned to write their pamphlets, select appropriate photographs, and draw pictures. At the computer lab, students typed in their copy and scanned their pictures. Once the pamphlets were assembled and copied, students distributed them around town and placed them in the library, supermarket, and other community centers.

Differentiating Instruction Through the Use of All the Styles

When it comes to learning styles, the ultimate learning goal is to achieve balance by developing ability in all four areas. One of the best ways to achieve this goal is to use a strategy called "Teaching Around the Wheel" (Silver & Hanson, 1998). In using this method, the teacher plans and delivers a series of instructional episodes in all four learning styles, thereby meeting the learning needs of all students and challenging students to master basic factual material (Mastery); think critically and analytically (Understanding); synthesize and apply information (Self-Expressive); and build on what they know personally (Interpersonal). As a result, student learning is deep, comprehensive, and memorable. For example, see Figure 2.9 for a Teaching Around the Wheel lesson on Countee Cullen's poem "Incident" (designed by Abigail Silver of Washington, D.C.).

Integrating Curriculum So That It Is Style-Rich and Style-Fair

Any curriculum provides multiple opportunities to incorporate style into student learning. By brainstorming options and ideas for your curricular themes, you can make sure your curriculum is robust and will engage all of your students. Start by listing ideas that will fit broadly into your curriculum. Once a number of ideas have been generated, select a few for each style that you think will work best in the curriculum (see Figure 2.10, p. 34). Develop and fine-tune your choices so that they will meet your instructional goals.

Providing Students with Choices in Activities and Assessments

An ideal strategy for diversifying assessment so that students have style-based options is Task Rotation (Silver, Hanson, Strong, & Schwartz, 1996). A Task Rotation consists of a menu of assessment activities correlated to style. The menu can be used in a number of ways depending on the teacher's purpose. For instance, students can be asked to:

• Complete all four activities in a specified sequence.

• Complete a certain number of activities in any sequence.

• Complete specific task(s) and choose others to complete.

• Choose the tasks they want to complete.

The Task Rotation in Figure 2.11 (p. 35) is taken from Joanne Curran's 3rd-grade classroom in Ladue, Missouri.

Carl Carrozza (1996), a 7th-grade science teacher in Catskill, New York, explains about this method of style-balanced assessment: "The Task Rotation provides a diversified structure for assessment. There are many different ways

FIGURE 2.9
TEACHING AROUND THE WHEEL

Mastery (Activity 2)	**Interpersonal** (Activity 1)
Organizing: Read the poem "Incident." Use the slide organizer to describe the incident. What happened before, during, and after the incident? **Memorizing:** Memorize the poem. **Reflecting:** Reflect on your process for memorizing the poem and identify what intelligences you used.	**Empathizing:** Describe a personal incident that changed the way you think and feel about things. Describe what happened before, during, and after the incident. Share your incident with a friend. Discuss some of the common characteristics of such incidents.
Understanding (Activity 3)	**Self-Expression** (Activity 4)
Interpreting: Read each of the statements. Decide if you agree or disagree. Cite particular lines in the poem to support or refute each statement. (The line may be interpreted literally or symbolically; e.g., May until December could be 8 months or a lifetime.) 1. The boy saw all of Baltimore. 2. The language of the poem is too simple. 3. The incident was completely destructive. 4. Confronting prejudice made the boy stronger.	**Metaphorical Expression:** List 5 things you know about prejudice. 1. 2. 3. 4. 5. **Select One:** How is prejudice like a shadow, tree, ice cube, whale, mirror, roller coaster?

FIGURE 2.10
CURRICULUM WHEEL

- **Graphic Organizer:** Students complete organizer during lecture on religion
- **Visualizing Vocabulary:** Selecting pictures that represent key words

- **Peer Practice:** Review in teams
- **Role Playing:** Empathizing with the Native Americans
- **Learning Circles**

Curriculum Theme:

Colonial America

- **Support and Refute:** Substantiate claims using readings on Anne Hutchinson and Amos Fortune.
- **Compare and Contrast:** Jamestown vs. Plymouth
- **Primary Document Learning:** Why was the death rate in Jamestown so high?

- **Metaphorical Expression:** How is a colony like a kaleidoscope?
- **Journal Writing**
- **Authentic Project:** Create a colonial comic strip.

to use it in the classroom, and students will find activities that play to their strengths and will be challenged by those they would normally avoid."

Supporting Student Learning in a Particular Style

Many teachers allow students to use another, more well-developed style to enhance their understanding of content, rather than insisting on following, say, the style of the Intuitive Thinker.

As with multiple intelligences, students who are weak in a particular area might be missing out on important content because there are few opportunities for them to learn according to their strengths. In fact, a study conducted by Hanson and Dewing (1990) of 2,000 learners shows that most at-risk students are unsuccessful not because they lack innate learning ability, but because their learning style is largely ignored in the classroom. Other research studies, includ-

ing those conducted by Dunn, Griggs, and Beasley (1995) and Carbo (1992), show that student achievement improves markedly when teachers address their students' learning styles.

Allowing students to work in their strong styles helps them build confidence in themselves as they acquire essential content that might otherwise elude them. A perfect example of the way a shift in style can improve achievement and build student confidence is found in the true story of an at-risk student named Michael who was having trouble mastering and understanding the structure of the Bill of Rights. The content had been presented to him in a Mastery-oriented way, as lists of Amendments to be remembered and to-the-point textbook prose to be read. Then, one day Michael was given the opportunity to learn the same content using his creative NF side, and a whole new picture of Michael's understanding "bloomed" before our eyes (see Figure 2.12, p. 36).

FIGURE 2.11
TASK ROTATION

Lions and Tigers and Bears & Mosquitoes

Our world is full of animals that are exciting and dangerous and annoying. Why are they here? Let's investigate. We would like all of us to select an irritating, powerful, or dangerous animal and explore its role in our world. When you think you know your animal well, select two of the challenges on this sheet to show what you have learned. We hope to include your work in our "Animals We Know" library.

Use your computer to construct a database for your animal.

Write a friendly letter explaining why you love your animal.

Develop a plan that will help preserve your animal and help others understand the role your animal plays in our world.

Create a myth to explain an important trait or behavior of your animal.

FIGURE 2.12
MICHAEL'S GARDEN OF BILL OF RIGHTS

Analyzing the Styles Used in Your Classroom

In reaching out to students of all four learning styles and in encouraging all students to become balanced, diverse learners, it is important that we provide them with the opportunity to work in all learning styles. In many cases, however, our own learning preferences dominate our classroom so that learners whose styles are different from our own become disengaged and unmotivated, while the learners whose styles match our own breeze through our assignments easily and without thinking deeply. Without even knowing it, we may be creating an environment where students find neither comfort nor challenge in our class-

rooms. For this reason, we must bring to the surface and analyze the ways in which we appeal or fail to appeal to different styles of learners with the work we assign and the instruction we provide.

To conduct your analysis and to develop on accurate representation of your classroom, review Figure 2.6, the style-dispositions chart (see p. 29). Next, examine Figure 2.13, which describes classroom activities and applications for each learning style. Collect examples from your teaching that use each of these learning styles. Identify the most and least represented styles in your classroom.

What do you need to do to create a style-balanced classroom?

FIGURE 2.13
COLLECTING CLASSROOM EXAMPLES

Intelligence	Examples of Classroom Activities	Examples from My Classroom

Mastery
Exercise—practice
	Direct instruction
	Drill and repetition
	Demonstrations
	Competitions
	Activities that focus on:
	  • organizing and managing information
	  • practicing a skill • observing
	  • describing • memorizing • categorizing	

Interpersonal
Experience—personalize
	Team games
	Learning circles
	Role playing
	Group investigation
	Peer tutoring
	Personal sharing
	Activities that focus on:
	  • describing feelings • empathizing
	  • responding • valuing	

Understanding
Explain—prove
	Inquiry
	Concept formation
	Debate
	Problem solving
	Independent study
	Essays
	Logic problems
	Activities that focus on:
	  • classifying • analyzing • using
	    evidence • applying • comparing
	    and contrasting • evaluating	

Self-Expressive
Explore—produce
	Divergent thinking
	Metaphors
	Creative art activities
	Imagining
	Open-ended discussion
	Imagery
	Creative problem solving
	Activities that focus on:
	  • hypothesizing • synthesizing
	  • symbolizing • creating • metaphorical
	    expression • self-expression	

Connecting the Models: Background

Intelligence, Style, and Four Famous Artists

WE BEGIN THIS CHAPTER WITH A LITTLE EXPERIMENT. Figures 3.1–3.4 show four famous pieces of art. Obviously, each of these artists has a highly developed spatial intelligence. But what about their styles? Which learning style might each artist represent?

The purpose of this experiment is to show how styles and intelligences are integrated. When you look at these four artists, it becomes clear that although all four demonstrate exceptional spatial intelligence, each has his own style.

• *Pablo Picasso's* provocative distortions of people and objects, known as cubism, reveal an artist breaking traditional modes of representation and attempting a new and unique form of painting. In breaking the mold of tradition, Picasso spent his career asking questions like these: What if I can show different realities at one time? What if I can make people think about art in new ways? What if I incorporate images of African art into Western painting? This desire to redirect the course of Western art represents a classic case of the Self-Expressive (NF) style.

• *Ansel Adams'* photographs of nature landscapes, on the other hand, are crystal-clear and precise black-and-white accounts of mountains, trees, deserts, and deserted roads, correlating with the Mastery (ST) style's premium on accuracy.

• *Norman Rockwell* used painting to communicate the funny and touching sentiments of family life and human experience. His nostalgic paintings of children and families have all the markings of the Interpersonal (SF) style.

• Finally, the way in which *M. C. Escher's* art uses optical illusions, symmetry, repeating patterns, and visual puzzles to explore the complex relationships between art, reality, and mathematics demonstrates the probing nature of the Understanding (NT) style.

The same idea holds true for all eight intelligences: For each intelligence, we can see four distinct ways of using that intelligence that correspond to the four learning styles. Consider the act of writing as another example. Figures 3.5–3.8 show four separate responses written by high school students to the question, "Why do you write?" See if you can tell which response represents which style of verbal-linguistic intelligence.

FIGURE 3.1–3.4
FOUR FAMOUS PIECES OF ART

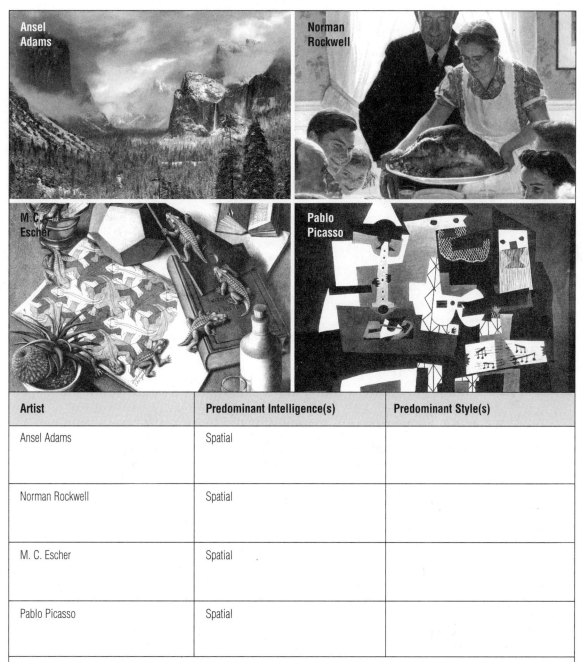

Artist	Predominant Intelligence(s)	Predominant Style(s)
Ansel Adams	Spatial	
Norman Rockwell	Spatial	
M. C. Escher	Spatial	
Pablo Picasso	Spatial	

Sources: Clockwise, from top left: **Ansel Adams:** Clearing Winter Storm in Yosemite National Park, © Ansel Adams Publishing Rights Trust/C; **Norman Rockwell:** Freedom from Want: Printed by permission of the Norman Rockwell Family Trust and the Norman Rockwell Museum, Stockbridge Massachusetts, and © 1943 the Norman Rockwell Family Trust; **Pablo Picasso:** Three Musicians: © 2000 Estate of Pablo Picasso / Artists Rights Society (ARS), New York, and photograph, © 2000 The Museum of Modern Art, New York; **M.C. Escher:** M.C. Escher's "Reptiles" © 1999 Cordon Art B.V.-Baarn - Holland. All rights reserved.

FIGURE 3.5–3.8
RESPONSES TO THE QUESTION "WHY DO YOU WRITE?"

Which response represents which *style* of verbal-linguistic intelligence (Mastery, Interpersonal, Understanding, or Self-Expressive)?

Response #1   Style _____

I used to write a lot when I was younger. I wrote notes to my friends. I kept a diary for a long time. I even wrote some poems. Every now and then I'd feel like I just had to write about the way I felt and what it might mean. I don't suppose it was very good, but I liked it. It was nice to know I could do that and it made me feel like I was getting to know myself better.

When I write I think a lot about whom I'm writing to and what I want to say and how I want them to feel. When I'm getting started I like to talk about what I'm going to do or sometimes I'll just stare off into space and doodle. And then I will get an idea and it all comes out in a gush. Sometimes when I look back on it, I hate it. But mostly what I write is okay. It sounds normal, like the way I talk.

The best thing I ever wrote was this poem about loneliness and roller-coasters and the people all around you screaming and you're still alone. I liked that poem a lot.

Response #2   Style _____

I'm always writing. I may not write it all down but I'm always writing. Even when I was very young there were always voices in my head, pictures in my mind. My mother would send me to the store and all the way home I'd be telling myself the story of my going to the store.

Writing is like the sea. That old wave of writing starts to build. You can feel it moving through every part of you, beating like a second heart, and then you're at the crest and you hold your breath and it just rolls out of you and all you can do is hold on and ride it out twisting and turning and watching things gleam and slide in the green water. And then you're up on the sand and half of the time you just want to walk away from it and the other half you can't wait to get out there and find another wave.

Response #3   Style _____

I write when I have to get the job done. Writing for me is neither pleasure nor pain. It's a job and I try to get it done as quickly as possible. I prefer writing assignments where the teacher tells me exactly what she wants and when she wants it.

For a big piece I'll usually begin by making a list of things I need to do. Then as I do them, I'll check them off. I don't believe in fancy outlines. I simply organize material in three groups: the beginning, the middle, and the end. Then I start writing. I like my first draft to be my last draft before recopying. I take a lot of time on recopying, making sure the pieces look good. I try to write in clear, simple language that doesn't force me to keep track of a lot of grammatical turns of phrase. The nicest thing a reader can say to me is that my writing is plain and clear and that my point is evident.

Response #4   Style _____

Writing has many purposes. You can use it to formulate new ideas, review material you have been studying, plan experiments or political activities, or persuade people over to your side. I write to think. That is to say, writing helps me focus my ideas so that they are more powerful.

My favorite kind of writing is editorial writing or persuasive essays. I begin by thinking of a provocative topic like euthanasia, and then by creating a question I want to explore, such as "Should euthanasia be legal?" Once I have a question, I collect lots of information that deals with many different positions on the issue. Usually by this time I have my own opinion. Then I make an outline for my essay which permits me to detach each of my subheadings (arguments for euthanasia, arguments against euthanasia, my opinion) and use each as the focus of a separate writing task. When I'm done writing, I go back to make sure everything's logical and well written.

Why Intelligence and Style Need Each Other

We can see how intelligences and styles are naturally and readily integrated by looking at the focal points of each model. Multiple-intelligence theory is centered around the *content* of learning and the relationship between learning and eight distinct fields of knowledge or disciplines. By focusing on content and disciplines of study, however, multiple-intelligence theory pays little attention to how people perceive and process information. The converse is true for learning styles: The style model revolves specifically around the individualized *process* of learning, but does not directly address the content of that learning. Clearly, learning styles and multiple intelligences need one another. Without multiple intelligences, learning styles cannot fully account for the content of learning. Without learning styles, multiple-intelligence theory is unable to account for different processes of thought and feeling. Each model responds directly to the limitations of the other (see Figure 3.9).

The distinct emphasis of each model becomes clear when we analyze variations within a particular intelligence. For example, conductors, performers, composers, and music critics all rely on a keenly developed musical intelligence to make their living, but are all of them using the same thinking processes (i.e., learning styles) in their use of musical intelligence? Aren't mechanics, dance critics, athletic coaches, and sculptors all using a bodily-kinesthetic intelligence, but in markedly different styles?

Most of us would agree that different styles of intelligence are operating in these individuals. Gardner would insist that personal histories and social contexts are key factors in explaining these differences, but how are teachers to differentiate their instruction according to such factors? Classroom teachers have to address differences in ways that are feasible, practical, and easy to implement. By focusing on how individuals think and feel, the learning-styles model proves just the tool needed to understand and teach to these differences. In this chapter, we show how we linked intelligences and styles so that teachers (or groups of teach-

FIGURE 3.9
THE CONTENT AND PROCESS OF LEARNING

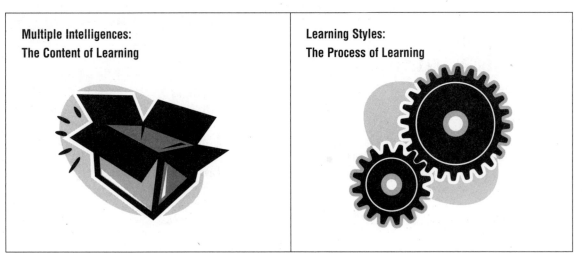

**Multiple Intelligences:
The Content of Learning**

**Learning Styles:
The Process of Learning**

ers) would be able to take full advantage of the relationships among intelligences and styles. We also describe four key principles that explain how the integration of styles and intelligences makes for sound, brain-based practice.

How We Integrated Multiple Intelligences and Learning Styles

In an *Educational Leadership* article entitled "Integrating Learning Styles and Multiple Intelligences" (Silver, Strong, & Perini, 1997), we described the process we used to connect the models. This method included three steps:

• **One:** Using intelligences as our starting point, we divided each intelligence four ways

according to each learning style. This means that for an intelligence (say, verbal-linguistic), four separate ways of using language were described (see Figure 3.10).

• **Two:** This step involved matching vocations and real-world applications to each intelligence–style profile. Drawing from a range of research exploring the relationship between psychological types and professions, such as Martin's (1997) *Looking at Types and Careers*, we listed professions that used each style-intelligence capability. In this way, intelligences and

FIGURE 3.10
STEP 1

MASTERY	INTERPERSONAL
The ability to use language to describe events and sequence activities	The ability to use language to build trust and rapport

VERBAL-LINGUISTIC

The ability to develop logical arguments and use rhetoric	The ability to use metaphoric and expressive language
UNDERSTANDING	**SELF-EXPRESSIVE**

FIGURE 3.11
STEP 2

MASTERY	INTERPERSONAL
The ability to use language to describe events and sequence activities	The ability to use language to build trust and rapport
Journalist *Technical Writer* *Administrator* *Contractor*	*Salesperson* *Counselor* *Clergyperson* *Therapist*

VERBAL-LINGUISTIC

The ability to develop logical arguments and use rhetoric	The ability to use metaphoric and expressive language
Lawyer *Professor* *Orator* *Philosopher*	*Playwright* *Poet* *Advertising Copywriter* *Novelist*
UNDERSTANDING	**SELF-EXPRESSIVE**

styles were situated firmly in the context of real-world applications (see Figure 3.11).

• **Three:** Finally, we collected descriptions of products an individual with a particular style–intelligence capability might create. To complete this step, we looked closely at the performance assessments used by teachers across the United States, fitting the products into the proper quadrant according to the intelligences and styles each assessment required students to use (see Figure 3.12).

Thus, we have created menus that provide teachers with a basis for an integrated assessment system that is easy to use. But before we dive into the implementation of this integrated learning model in the classroom, let's explore the overriding principles that direct our endeavor into integrated education.

The Principles of Diversity

Encouraging diversity while simultaneously making sure that all students can meet state and national standards is a goal in nearly every

FIGURE 3.12
STEP 3

	MASTERY	INTERPERSONAL	
Write an article	The ability to use language to describe events and sequence activities	The ability to use language to build trust and rapport	Write a letter
Put together a magazine			Make a pitch
Develop a plan			Conduct an interview
Develop a newscast	*Journalist Technical Writer Administrator Contractor*	*Salesperson Counselor Clergyperson Therapist*	Counsel a fictional character or a friend
Describe a complex procedure/object			
	VERBAL-LINGUISTIC		
Make a case	The ability to develop logical arguments and use rhetoric	The ability to use metaphoric and expressive language	Write a play
Make/defend a decision			Develop a plan to direct
Advance a theory			Spin a tale
Interpret a text	*Lawyer Professor Orator Philosopher*	*Playwright Poet Advertising Copywriter Novelist*	Develop an advertising campaign
Explain an artifact			
	UNDERSTANDING	SELF-EXPRESSIVE	

43

classroom. Yet it seems as though many teachers find these two demands (the demand for diversity and the demand for standards-based learning) to be at odds with one another. We know that we can encourage a full range of diversity with two powerful learning models: learning styles and multiple intelligences. And we know that these two models can, and should, be integrated into a holistic model of learning. Putting this model into practice in a way that will maximize achievement means that we need to pay attention to four key principles: comfort, challenge, depth, and motivation. These principles are guided by what current brain research tells us about getting the most out of the learning process. So as we begin to apply our integrated model of learning to instruction, to assessment, and to curriculum, these principles of diversity should serve as guidelines both for implementation and for evaluating the results along the way.

Principle 1: Comfort

Building comfort into learning is essential if we expect students to respond positively and constructively to their education. As brain researcher Eric Jensen (1996) explains,

> When a student feels helpless in the face of a learning experiment, or even subtly threatened by an assignment, a defense trigger is pulled in the brain. The learner reacts and goes into a state of stress. In some cases, the threat may be perceived as indirectly aimed at one's self-esteem, confidence, and peer acceptance (p. 87).

Obviously, a state of extreme discomfort in a learning situation is detrimental to quality education.

How comfortable students feel has a lot to do with styles and intelligences. As we know, not everybody is comfortable with the same thing. In fact, what makes one person comfortable often makes another person uneasy and restless.

Thus, it is important to create comfort by employing learning activities in each of the four style neighborhoods and in a wide range of intelligences. Part of effective teaching is matching strategies and assessment activities to students' learning profiles, thereby making students feel more comfortable in the classroom.

Principle 2: Challenge

Learning, as Vygotsky (1978) tells us, means being ready to be challenged; we grow as learners by reaching beyond our current abilities. And though discomfort is detrimental to learning and building comfort is important, optimal learning requires more than just comfort. If too extreme, comfort can lead to uncritical contentedness and mental laziness. Instead, as renowned psychologist Mihaly Csikszentmihalyi (1990) has noted, optimal learning occurs during a mental state called "flow." Central to flow is the idea of comfort tempered by challenge in such a way that the mind becomes lost in the performance and naturally seeks to apply itself to a nonthreatening, but mentally demanding task.

From the standpoint of learning styles and multiple intelligences, encouraging this optimal learning state means finding the right balance of comfort and challenge. Students will accept a challenge if they feel that teachers respect and value their dominant styles and intelligences. If not, students may be unwilling to challenge themselves by working in those styles and intelligences that need developing. Because good teaching, over a period of weeks or months, uses activities in all four styles and all eight intelligences, it naturally creates comfort and simultaneously provides opportunities for students to be challenged and stretched. Exposing students to strategies and activities that are not of their dominant styles and intelligences not only makes them stronger, more balanced, and more flexible learners, but also makes them more tolerant of those who do things differently.

Principle 3: Depth

Have you ever heard a teacher say, "But I've got to cover the content"? From the perspective of brain research, few approaches could be more antithetical to the way the brain learns than the predominant cycle of content coverage: Teach, quiz, teach, quiz, teach, unit test. As Jensen (1996) explains,

> For most learners school consists of larger complex topics that have been chunked down, dumbed down, watered down, and thinned out. It's often boring when a topic or unit is reduced to the lowest common denominator, the smallest information chunk teachable. It's in a chunk, chunk, chunk, chunk, then end format. The brain learns poorly this way (p. 103).

What is desired instead is an approach that allows for "more time, more depth with fewer, more complex topics" (Jensen, 1996, p. 103). Both learning styles and multiple intelligences meet the demands of this brain-based approach. Depth of learning comes as students process and think more intently about the content from various perspectives and in many lights. Implementing activities and strategies in all styles and intelligences naturally encourages students to commit to topics in a deeper, more meaningful way and enables them to handle complex topics with greater ease. As such, the foundation on which new content can be built will be stronger and longer lasting.

Principle 4: Motivation

The word *boring* has its roots in an Old English word meaning to drill using the same motion over and over. When faced with constant repetition, we become bored—and we become unmotivated. Similarly, students who are forced to learn in the same way day after day can become bored and lose their motivation for learning.

As we all know, repetition is a poor motivator. Studies on the roles of teacher control and student choice in learning show that self-motivation on the part of students can be expected only if students have opportunities to focus on topics and activities that interest them (Glasser, 1985; Mager & McCann, 1963). By putting diversity to work with learning styles and multiple intelligences, teachers create a classroom environment in which students are engaged in finding their own talents and interests. Through personal exploration and the ability to choose, students remain interested, participate actively, build self-confidence, and develop the self-motivation needed to become good learners.

Having these principles as a benchmark, we are ready to begin the practical journey into style-and-intelligence-integrated curriculum, instruction, and assessment.

Integrated Curriculum, Integrated Instruction

JOHN GOODLAD, IN HIS LANDMARK RESEARCH STUDY *A Place Called School* (1984), described a typical school day like this:

> I stood in the open doorway of a classroom of one of the junior high schools we studied. It was one of a series of classes located side by side down a long hallway. The day was a warm one and the doors of three of the classrooms were open. Inside each, the teacher sat at a desk, watching the class or reading. The students sat at table-type desks arranged in rows. Most were writing, a few were stretching, and the remainder were looking contemplatively or blankly into space. In one of two other rooms with closed doors, the students were watching a film. It appeared to be on the cause and prevention of soil erosion. In the other, the teacher was putting an algebraic equation on the chalkboard and explaining its components to the class. In visits to several other academic classes that day, I witnessed no marked variations on these pedagogical procedures and student activities (p. 93).

To be sure, not all classrooms operate in the way Goodlad describes, with the premium placed on content coverage and independent seatwork at the expense of diverse and engaging learning opportunities. Moreover, many educators today are exploring ways to encourage active learning and discourage student passivity: problem-based learning; performance assessment; teaching for understanding; and style-, intelligence-, and brain-compatible instruction. Yet the fact remains that most teachers still feel intense pressure to cover the content and may consequently miss opportunities to help students become deep, multifaceted thinkers and learners.

Traditionally, our schools have concentrated primarily on Mastery (ST) and Understanding (NT) learning styles (Hanson & Dewing, 1990), along with verbal-linguistic and logical-mathematical intelligences (Armstrong, 1994). This gravitation toward specific styles and intelligences makes it difficult for students with other styles and dominant intelligences to relate to what they learn. For instance, a student with a dominant Interpersonal (SF) style and a strong orientation for bodily-kinesthetic intelligence will almost certainly have difficulty maintaining interest in a textbook assignment that requires working alone and answering questions at the end of the chapter. On the other hand, by catering to those students whose styles and intelligences correlate with those privileged by our schools, we deny these students the opportunity to think in new ways and to grow by being challenged.

Teachers need to create a classroom environment that allows students to process information the way they do in the world outside of school. Outside school, children tend to rely on their natural ways of learning. In school, however, we often ask students to process in only one or two ways. This significantly inhibits their ability to grasp the concepts and skills they need to learn to construct a substantial and permanent base of knowledge. Moreover, the preponderance of one or two styles and one or two intelligences in our schools prevents students from developing what Goodlad (1984) refers to as the "full range of intellectual abilities" (p. 93) demanded and valued in the worlds of work and citizenship that await them after school.

Two Classroom Scenarios

To begin our exploration of style- and intelligence-fair curriculum and instruction, let's look inside two classrooms.

Scenario One: Teaching for Intelligences

William Massimo, a middle school math teacher in Teaneck, New Jersey, designed a lesson on the Fibonacci Sequence (a famous mathematical sequence developed by the Italian mathematician Fibonacci in which each term is the sum of the previous two terms: 1, 1, 2, 3, 5, 8, 13, 21 . . .) using his knowledge of multiple intelligences. To spur students to tap into a wide range of intelligences, William knew he would need to diversify his instructional approaches. Figure 4.1 summarizes how he did it. (Note, again, the abbreviations used here and elsewhere for the eight intelligences: V = verbal-linguistic; L = logical-mathematical; S = spatial; M = musical; B = bodily-kinesthetic; P = interpersonal; I = intrapersonal; N = naturalist.)

FIGURE 4.1

INTELLIGENCES ANALYSIS OF WILLIAM'S LESSON

V	• Lecture • Notemaking techniques
L	• Find values of 9th, 10th, 11th, and 12th terms • Develop an equation
S	• Graphing
M	• (None)
B	• Manipulatives
P	• Working with a partner
I	• Tracking personal progress in learning log
N	• Slides of pine trees

Note: Intelligence abbreviations: V = verbal-linguistic; L = logical-mathematical; S = spatial; M = musical; B = bodily-kinesthetic; P = interpersonal; I = intrapersonal; N = naturalist.

To engage verbal-linguistic intelligence, William delivered a lecture on number sequences and the Fibonacci Sequence, asking students to take notes using a variety of note-taking strategies. For the naturalist intelligence, William showed students slides of pine trees and asked students to think about the relation between the Fibonacci Sequence and nature. After students made and discussed their hypotheses, William described how Fibonacci derived his famous sequence by studying the shapes of pine trees. Next, William asked students to work with a partner to discover the pattern of the Fibonacci Sequence, to find the values of the 9th, 10th, 11th, and 12th terms, and to develop an equation to find the value of any number in the pattern, thereby engaging both logical-mathematical and interpersonal intelligences. For developing spatial intelligence, he asked students to graph the coordinates of the sequence. Bodily-kinesthetic intelligence was employed by having students work with manipulatives to physically represent the sequence. Finally, to engage intrapersonal intelligence, William asked students to keep track of their personal progress and to express what they learned and what questions they still had in their learning logs. The lesson sequence ended with a mastery test to ensure students understood the Fibonacci Sequence and could apply their learning.

Scenario Two: Teaching for Learning Styles

Eva Benevento's primary model for diversity is learning styles. In developing an instructional unit on Greek mythology for her 5th graders in Teaneck, she identified the learning goals for her lesson according to styles, as follows:

• *Mastery:* My students will be able to identify the components of mythology.

• *Understanding:* My students will be able to explain how Greek mythology and Greek culture are interrelated.

• *Self-Expressive:* My students will be able to appreciate and understand Greek mythology as art by creating their own myths.

• *Interpersonal:* My students will be able to understand how myths are universal and how the themes apply to their own lives.

In planning and implementing her lesson, she paid close attention to each of her learning-style goals and developed lessons and activities around each of these (for a summary, see Figure 4.2). To meet her Mastery goal (*Students will be able to identify the components of mythology*), Eva

delivered an interactive lecture explaining the components of mythology and providing an overview of Greek culture. To deepen students' memories and content knowledge, she provided them with a visual organizer to record key information from the lecture into appropriate slots.

FIGURE 4.2
STYLE ANALYSIS OF EVA'S LESSON

MASTERY	INTERPERSONAL
• Interactive lecture • Graphic Organizer	• Socratic Seminar • Discuss two mythology themes in terms of your own life
• Support and refute statements • Essay **UNDERSTANDING**	• Identify aesthetic components • Create myth of a current-events figure **SELF-EXPRESSIVE**

In reading a selection of myths, students were provided with a group of statements keyed to the relationship between Greek culture and mythology. Students were asked to support and refute these statements using evidence from the texts. In this way, Eva was able to meet her Understanding goal (*Students will be able to explain how Greek mythology and Greek culture are interrelated*). To further meet her Understanding goal, she had students prepare a brief essay explaining how this interrelationship plays out in two myths of their own choice.

The Self-Expressive goal (*Students will be able to appreciate and understand Greek mythology as art by creating their own myths)* presented a wonderful opportunity to focus on the aesthetics of Greek mythology. In small groups and as a whole class, students identified aesthetic components (metaphors, similes, hyperbole, style, characterization, personification, imagery) of mythology and developed a working explanation of how these devices and components affected them as readers. A whole-class discussion led to the creation of a chart, recorded by Eva and copied by the students, which outlined aesthetic components and their effects. Using this chart as a guide, students then created their own myths by focusing on a figure in current events and telling his or her story in mythical terms.

Finally, to meet the Interpersonal goal (*Students will understand how myths are universal and how the themes apply to their own lives*), Eva asked students to conduct a Socratic Seminar focused on the question: "What makes mythology universal?" After the discussion, students culminated their learning by selecting two common themes from mythology (e.g., overcoming challenges) and writing essays about these themes in terms of their own lives.

Analysis and Integration

These two classroom scenarios represent the work of two excellent teachers who are concerned with reaching all students through a range of instructional activities. William Massimo designed his lesson around multiple intelligences, whereas Eva Benevento planned her lesson unit with the four learning styles in mind. When we combine the planning formats used by each teacher, we form a matrix that can be used to audit our current lessons and units according to styles and intelligences to determine how well different teaching strategies meet our instructional objectives, and to design lessons that combine the insights of our two great models of human differences. Figure 4.3 pro-

vides a framework for such an analysis.

Such an integration may seem to conflict with what is a somewhat common feeling among teachers who value diversity: the use of one learning model often occurs at the expense of the other model. But integrating both models into curriculum and instruction is not only essential if we are to commit ourselves to the true meaning of diversity, it is also something that can be done without significantly changing current practices or placing excessive burden on teachers—even if they are newcomers to learning styles and multiple intelligences.

As style- and intelligence-fair teacher Carl Carrozza of Catskill, New York (1996), explains on integrating the models:

> I found that as I used learning styles in my classroom, students became increasingly engaged because there were opportunities for them to learn science content according to their own styles as learners ....

> More recently, I have become interested in the application of Howard Gardner's theory of multiple intelligences. Multiple intelligence theory gives me a clear model for connecting various fields and disciplines. With the help of Gardner's model, I have found it possible to link learning between disciplines so that students who love music, for example, might be able to explore the scientific concepts of a piano or a series of soundwaves that create melody, while the athlete might understand how an exercise regimen is scientifically grounded (p. 146).

Through the fusion of learning styles, multiple intelligences, and effective lesson planning and implementation, teachers can promote the highest levels of active, in-depth learning in the classroom, while also making success a reality for every student. The first step in creating this fusion is auditing and realigning curriculum.

FIGURE 4.3
COMBINING THE MODELS

V	
L	
S	
M	
B	
P	
I	
N	

MASTERY	INTERPERSONAL
UNDERSTANDING	SELF-EXPRESSIVE

	MASTERY	UNDERSTANDING	SELF-EXPRESSIVE	INTERPERSONAL
V				
L				
S				
M				
B				
P				
I				
N				

Note: V = verbal-linguistic; L = logical-mathematical; S = spatial; M = musical; B = bodily- kinesthetic; P = interpersonal; I = intrapersonal; N = naturalist intelligence.

50

Curriculum Auditing and Realignment

The Virtue of Renovation

A good curriculum unit is like a house: Each calls for a solid foundation; each requires a well-thought-out design; and each is built into a useful and lasting finished product. But not all houses and not all curricula are built from scratch. Sometimes a solid structure has already been built, making it counterproductive to tear it down and start again each time a fault is discovered.

We begin this section with the metaphor of a house because we want to highlight the virtue of renovation. Because so much time and energy goes into planning curriculum units, it is not always feasible or wise to send them to the scrap heap whenever new learning shows the wear of an old model. Often, simple renovations or additions can make a world of difference. The maxim warning against the foolishness of

reinventing the wheel, of wasting valuable resources to do what has already been done ably, is often true in the case of curriculum: Developing style–intelligence integrated curriculum need not be an act of tearing down to start over—it is often a matter of making powerful adjustments to an already existing foundation.

Steps to Follow

Incorporating learning styles and multiple intelligences into a curriculum unit begins with an audit of an existing unit. Out of the audit comes an analysis, and from the analysis emerges a plan for integration. Auditing and realigning curriculum are achieved through a simple, five-step process:

Step 1: Think about a lesson or unit you have already planned. Identify, in simple language, the standards you are addressing or the outcomes you wish to achieve. (See Figures 4.4 and 4.5 for elementary and secondary school examples.)

FIGURE 4.4
SAMPLE OUTCOME: ELEMENTARY SCHOOL

Elementary Example: Vocabulary Unit

Students will learn:
- To improve their power over new words
- To use context clues to define a word
- To demonstrate their understanding of word meanings
- To express themselves clearly in writing and speech

FIGURE 4.5
SAMPLE OUTCOME: SECONDARY SCHOOL

Secondary Example: A Unit on Order of Operations

Students will:
- Review basic operations and formulas
- Master order of operations
- Use estimation to check work
- Input order of operations problems into a calculator
- Apply mathematical formulas for area, perimeter, volume, and price
- Engage in problem solving, planning, cooperative work, and creative thinking

Step 2: List the assessment tasks, processing activities, and instructional episodes students will engage in throughout the unit.

(See Figures 4.6 and 4.7 for elementary and secondary activities, respectively.)

FIGURE 4.6
ELEMENTARY ACTIVITIES

Assessments	Processing Activities / Instructional Episodes
Task Rotation **(M)** Mark the word that best completes the phrase. **(U)** Complete analogies. **(S)** Create a sentence chain or paragraph using as many vocabulary words as students can. **(I)** Peer Practice—coaching partnerships for selecting antonyms and synonyms **Summarize the Piece**	**Do you hear what I hear?** Text: *The Great Kapok Tree: A Tale of the Amazon Rainforest* After listening to and reading the selection, students review words using this code: _____ familiar words (vaguely familiar * unfamiliar **Pretest—What do you think?** Students write what they think each word means using context clues. **Compare and Contrast** Initial definitions with dictionary definitions **Visualizing the Word** Create four pictures that represent each word and write a specific sentence explaining why the pictures are good examples. **Inductive Learning** Group and label words

Note: Style abbreviations: M = Mastery style; U = Understanding style; S = Self-expressive style; I = Interpersonal style.

FIGURE 4.7
SECONDARY ACTIVITIES

Assessments	Processing Activities / Instructional Episodes
1. King Arthur Wants You! King Arthur needs a fence that will enclose his entire grounds. Help him figure out how much fencing is necessary by finding the perimeter of the grounds. *Take Note:* **HE DOES NOT** wish to separate the castle grounds from the hunting grounds with fencing. a) Can parentheses be used in your expression? _____ b) If so, how? _____ c) Are parentheses necessary? _____ d) Why or why not? _____ Find the area of King Arthur's grounds. a) Did your equation to find the area use parentheses? _____ b) Why or why not? _____ **2. LET'S GO SHOPPING!** (Culminating Assessment) You and your sibling have decided to redecorate your room. **Required purchases:** 2 beds, sheets, pillows, blankets, floor covering (your room is 20' by 20'), 2 desks, floor lamp, ceiling lights. Your parents will pay for the above purchases, plus half of whatever else you buy as long as they do not spend more than $1,500 total. The only conditions are that you: • use the included catalog. • write up a plan showing what you will buy and spend. The cost of everything should be expressed in a single equation. DO NOT estimate and DO NOT forget the order of operations. **Mastery Test** **Homework** **Class Participation**	**Hook: Connect the Dots** What is needed for everyone to connect the dots the same way? **How is it possible?** Two candy store problems—same equation, two different answers **Discussion** Does order matter? Batting order in baseball. **New American Lecture** Order of operations in a recipe format **Memory Aid** Use the first letter of each word to create a memorable sentence: Parentheses, Exponent, Multiply or Divide, Add or Subtract **Step-by-Step Practice** **Self-Assessment** **Independent Practice** **Peer Practice** Students coach each other through the process **Journal Writing** How is an eggshell like a set of parentheses? **Technology Education** Estimation versus Calculation

Step 3: Use the Learning Styles–Multiple Intelligences Matrix to analyze those styles and intelligences you are already addressing in your curriculum. (See Figures 4.8 and 4.9 for sample elementary and secondary matrixes, respectively. Note that activities and instructional episodes may be placed in more than one box.)

FIGURE 4.8
ELEMENTARY MATRIX

	MASTERY	UNDERSTANDING	SELF-EXPRESSIVE	INTERPERSONAL
V	Complete sentences Summarize piece	Analogies	Sentence chain Inductive Learning	Peer Practice Generate own definitions
L		Analogies Compare and Contrast definitions	Inductive Learning	
S	Using code to review words	Visualizing vocabulary	Visualizing vocabulary	
M				
B				
P				Peer Practice
I			Pretest—generate own definitions	
N				

Note: V = verbal-linguistic; L = logical-mathematical; S = spatial; M = musical; B = bodily- kinesthetic; P = interpersonal; I = intrapersonal; N = naturalist intelligence.

FIGURE 4.9
SECONDARY MATRIX

	MASTERY	UNDERSTANDING	SELF-EXPRESSIVE	INTERPERSONAL
V	Peer Practice Step-by-Step Practice New American Lecture Mastery Test	Journal	Journal Memory Aid Math and Baseball	Journal Discussion Class Participation
L		Technology: Calculation vs. Estimation Discussion Hook	Math and Baseball	Peer Practice Let's Go Shopping
S	New American Lecture	King Arthur Wants You Let's Go Shopping		
M				
B				
P	Peer Practice	Discussion		Class Participation
I	Independent Practice	Independent Practice		Self-Assessment Independent Practice
N				

Note: V = verbal-linguistic; L = logical-mathematical; S = spatial; M = musical; B = bodily- kinesthetic; P = interpersonal; I = intrapersonal; N = naturalist intelligence.

Step 4: Based on your analysis, generate some ideas on what kinds of intelligences and styles you need to address. (For elementary and secondary examples of teachers' ideas, see Figures 4.10 and 4.11, respectively.)

see Figures 4.10 and 4.11, respectively.

FIGURE 4.10
TEACHER'S IDEAS: ELEMENTARY SCHOOL

Elementary Example

After her analysis, this teacher wrote:

I used all the styles well. Aside from the verbal-linguistic intelligence, which is central to the unit, I also used spatial (Visualizing Vocabulary), intrapersonal (students generate own definitions), interpersonal (Peer Practice), and logical-mathematical (analogies) intelligences.

In the past I have had students perform "concept skits" to act out ideas. Maybe I should do this for definitions to work in bodily kinesthetic intelligence. I could also have students select music that matches a word's meaning to promote musical intelligence.

Step 5: Review and implement your ideas. If possible, discuss your changes and plans with fellow teachers, and use their feedback to further improve your new guidelines.

It's always best to do curriculum work in a group. Many school districts are eager to support this work if it focuses on improved instruction, inclusion of standards, and better assessment. Working with other 3rd grade teachers or math teachers allows you to divide

some of the tasks, as well as use each other's preferred or strongest intelligences and styles.

Use the ideas on instruction, instructional units, and assessment that follow to help you develop a better instructional program.

FIGURE 4.11
TEACHER'S IDEAS: SECONDARY SCHOOL

Secondary Example

After his analysis, this teacher wrote:

My unit is pretty well integrated already. I've got all the styles included, and five of eight intelligences. Of course, it isn't necessary to get all the intelligences into every unit, but I have an idea about getting musical intelligence in easily: I could change the discussion question about batting order into a question about musical composition:
- introduction
- verse
- chorus
- verse
- chorus
- bridge
- verse
- chorus

Integrated Instruction

Active, in-depth learning is a goal in most classrooms across the United States. Yet researchers as diverse as school investigator John Goodlad (1984), former secretary of labor Robert Reich (1992), assessment expert Grant Wiggins (1993), brain researcher Eric Jensen (1996), and others have all pointed out that many classrooms are bogged down with covering content in ways that treat students as passive receptacles of information. In truth, we know more than ever before about how students learn and how to motivate and involve students. Too often these ideas are not being implemented successfully in our classrooms. This conclusion raises a complex question: How do teachers create learning-compatible classrooms that engage all types of learners; that teach essential content and develop essential skills; and that make use of effective techniques to motivate students and enhance their learning? The answer to this question is *integrated instruction*. Integrated instruction implies three components:

* The incorporation of multiple intelligences into teaching.
* The incorporation of learning styles into teaching.
* The incorporation of successful, research-based instructional strategies into teaching.

In terms of building a repertoire of instructional strategies, a number of invaluable resources will help. Books like *Models of Teaching* (Joyce & Weil, 1996), *A Different Kind of Classroom: Teaching with Dimensions of Learning* (Marzano, 1992), *Teaching Styles and Strategies* (Silver, Hanson, Strong, & Schwartz, 1996), and video libraries such as Canter and Associates' *Developing Lifelong Learners* (1996), Video Journal's *Instructional Strategies for Greater Student Achievement* (1995), and ASCD's *Teaching Strategies Library* (1987) provide teachers with practical, research-based techniques they can implement in their classroom. Each of these programs is based on an overarching model of learning that shows teachers how to diversify their instructional practice, meet the needs of various learners, and respond to the demands of life in the classroom through the use of instructional strategies.

To explain how to integrate strategies, intelligences, and styles into instruction, we would like to introduce you to four teachers. These teachers know that learning styles and multiple intelligences serve as tools to analyze particular teaching strategies to determine how well a strategy will meet instructional objectives. For example, the teacher who wishes to develop critical thinking skills would likely look for strategies that emphasize logical-mathematical intelligence and the Understanding style. For the teacher who is interested in increasing students' personal involvement, strategies focusing on interpersonal and intrapersonal intelligences and Interpersonal style would be most useful.

Operating this way, teachers can avoid the common trap of randomly peppering a lesson with styles and intelligences, and instead concentrate instruction around their students' needs by understanding how the strategies they use enlist appropriate styles and intelligence. Unlike the process of curriculum auditing described earlier, which is a general process for identifying styles and intelligences, strategy analysis entails a more fine-tuned search for style and intelligence connections. The analysis of any teaching strategy can be performed using the integrated matrix (see Figure 4.9, p. 55).

Now, let's meet our four teachers and observe their approaches to integrated instruction:

Scenario One: 11th Grade English

Robin Cederblad of Downer's Grove, Illinois, realized that many of the problems her 11th grade English literature students had in reading texts stemmed from their inability to construct images of what they were reading and make effective predictions about their readings. To help students overcome these difficulties, she began using a strategy known as "Mind's Eye" (Brownlie & Silver, 1995, adapted from Escondido School District, 1979). Currently, she is using Mind's Eye to help students develop and employ visualizing skills while reading a chapter from Dickens's *A Tale of Two Cities*. Robin selects a list of keywords and phrases from the chapter (see Figure 4.12).

FIGURE 4.12
DICKENS'S KEYWORDS

storms	downstairs	horses	ball	snuff
courtyard	carriage	escaping	streets	dispersed
cry	narrow	knitting	loud	killed
recklessness	screaming	watchfulness	wrong	child
contemptuous	silent	eyes	"Go on!"	shrieked
coin	dignity	desperation	dead	fancy
purse	pay			

Robin reads these words aloud slowly, with emphasized emotion, and encourages students to construct mental images of what might be happening in the story. As she reads each word, she asks students to add to and refine their images. After the visualizing phase, students must do one of four things:

• Draw a picture based on their visualizations.

• Formulate a question they hope the text will answer.

• Make a prediction about the text.

• Describe the feelings the words and mental images called forth.

Robin asks students to share their products with other students and to discuss what they believe the reading will provide or how it will unfold. Students then read the chapter independently and discuss how their predictions compare with the actual text. Robin's analysis is shown in Figure 4.13.

Scenario Two: 4th Grade Math

For Susan Daniels of Teaneck, helping her 4th grade students learn, internalize, and apply the process of solving fraction problems often proved a source of difficulty because the rules students had been learning for four years about whole numbers suddenly did not apply anymore. Rather than simply listing and repeating steps through drill and practice sessions, Susan began looking for ways to increase her students' personal engagement with the content and with their fellow classmates. In her search for a teaching strategy suitable to these objectives, she discovered "Peer Practice" (Silver et al., 1996, adapted from Mosston, 1972). Now, after modeling the problem-solving process, Susan supplements direct instruction with Peer Practice sessions, in which pairs of students are given worksheets like the ones shown in Figures 4.14 and 4.15 (see p. 60).

Each student in the partnership solves his problems while his partner, who has the answers and a list of the steps in the procedure, coaches him through areas of difficulty. Each team also has access to a set of manipulatives, which learners may use to help represent the problem.

FIGURE 4.13
ROBIN'S ANALYSIS OF THE MIND'S EYE STRATEGY

	MASTERY	UNDERSTANDING	SELF-EXPRESSIVE	INTERPERSONAL
V	Listen carefully to the words			Describe a feeling
L		Formulate a question	Make a prediction	
S	Draw a picture	Compare pre-reading images with text	Construct mental images	
M				
B				
P	Discuss pre-reading ideas			Share products
I	Independent reading			Describe a feeling
N				

Note: V = verbal-linguistic; L = logical-mathematical; S = spatial; M = musical; B = bodily- kinesthetic; P = interpersonal; I = intrapersonal; N = naturalist intelligence.

As students work on each problem, they must think aloud so that their problem-solving process is revealed to themselves and their coaches. Susan emphasizes that coaching involves providing hints, suggestions, and positive feedback, but not giving answers: Each student must come to the solution on her own. When both students have solved their problems and coached one another, they work together to solve the cooperative challenge at the bottom of the worksheet that forecasts the next lesson: mixed numerals (see Figure 4.16, p. 61 for

FIGURE 4.14
PARTNER 1'S WORKSHEET

Your problems	Answers to your partner's problems
1. 2/3 + 5/8	1. 37/30
2. 3/7 + 11/14	2. 13/15
3. 1/4 + 1/6	3. 5/4
4. 2/3 – 1/6	4. 1/4
5. 2/3 – 1/9	5. 5/9

Remembering the steps:

1. Find lowest common denominator (LCD)
2. Use LCD to make like fractions
3. Add or subtract
4. Write answer in lowest terms

Cooperative Challenge!
If 2/3 = 2/3, and 3/3 = 1, what does 4/3 equal?

Hint, your answer will be a number greater than 1.

FIGURE 4.15
PARTNER 2'S WORKSHEET

Your problems	Answers to your partner's problems
1. 5/6 + 2/5	1. 31/24
2. 1/5 + 2/3	2. 17/14
3. 9/10 + 7/20	3. 5/12
4. 3/4 - 1/2	4. 1/2
5. 8/9 - 1/3	5. 5/9

Remembering the steps:

1. Find lowest common denominator (LCD)
2. Use LCD to make like fractions
3. Add or subtract
4. Write answer in lowest terms

Cooperative Challenge!
If 2/3 = 2/3, and 3/3 = 1, what does 4/3 equal?

Hint, your answer will be greater than 1.

Susan's analysis). After just a few sessions, students' cooperative skills and mathematical understanding improve markedly.

Scenario Three: 2nd Grade Social Studies

When she wants to help her 2nd grade students identify with historical figures and feel the importance of significant events, Linda Diskin of Teaneck uses the "Simulation Strategy." Linda has found the core of the strategy—role playing—is an extremely effective learning tool that helps develop students' powers of insight, observation, self-understanding, and empathy (see Linda's analysis in Figure 4.17, p. 62). For her current lesson on Thanksgiving, Linda asked all of her students to bring in their favorite piece of fruit and had a few students explain why they like their fruit. Linda surveyed and recorded student responses, which included:

- It tastes good.
- It's sweet.
- My mom says it gives people energy.
- It's good for you.

After establishing that people need food like

FIGURE 4.16
SUSAN'S ANALYSIS OF THE PEER PRACTICE STRATEGY

	MASTERY	UNDERSTANDING	SELF-EXPRESSIVE	INTERPERSONAL
V				Listening to coach Coaching partner
L	Practice solving problems			Cooperative challenge
S				
M				
B		Manipulatives	Manipulatives	
P			Cooperative challenge	Developing coaching skills
I			Using and applying coach's feedback Think Alouds	Think Alouds (Explaining internal thinking process during problem solving)
N				

Note: V = verbal-linguistic; L = logical-mathematical; S = spatial; M = musical; B = bodily- kinesthetic; P = interpersonal; I = intrapersonal; N = naturalist intelligence.

fruit to survive, Linda told the students they would take turns acting out a major event in American history—the first Thanksgiving. She began the lesson by reviewing the information they had already learned about the meeting between the Pilgrims and the Native Americans.

Linda then explained that five students would act as Native Americans, and that these five students would have all of the fruit. When Linda asked students to guess why one group had so much fruit, one student responded, "Because they knew how to grow things." Linda said,

FIGURE 4.17
LINDA'S ANALYSIS OF THE SIMULATION STRATEGY

	MASTERY	UNDERSTANDING	SELF-EXPRESSIVE	INTERPERSONAL
V		Discussion		Discussion
L				
S				
M				
B			Role playing (physical acting)	
P				Role playing (interacting)
I		Observing/interpreting Role playing	Role playing (personal response to situations)	Empathizing
N	Basic understanding of food/nourishment			

Note: V = verbal-linguistic; L = logical-mathematical; S = spatial; M = musical; B = bodily- kinesthetic; P = interpersonal; I = intrapersonal; N = naturalist intelligence.

"That's correct," and further explained that since the Native Americans were expert hunters and farmers, they usually had enough food to eat. Linda then asked five students to come to the center of the learning circle and act out what they knew about Native American life.

Next, Linda discussed the arrival of the Pilgrims in North America, focusing especially on how they were unaccustomed to this new land and how they did not have enough food to survive. She then selected five students to join the Native Americans and to act out what they knew about Pilgrim life (i.e., that they were cold and hungry). When the Pilgrim group explained how hungry they were, the Native American group shared their fruit with them and showed them how they planted food.

After the role playing, Linda involved the entire class in discussion. She asked students to talk about what it felt like to act out their roles and to watch the action take place, using the following questions to guide and deepen their discussion:

• How would the Native Americans feel about the Pilgrims coming to their homeland? How would they feel when they found out how little food the Pilgrims had?

• How would the Pilgrims feel arriving in a strange, new land with so little food?

• How did it feel to play each role?

• How did it feel to watch some of the events of the first Thanksgiving?

• What else do you know about the earliest Thanksgiving that was celebrated?

• Are any of these traditions still celebrated today?

Over the course of the year, Linda uses "Simulation" several more times, especially when it comes time to discuss how the Native Americans had their land taken away from them.

Scenario Four: 7th Grade Science

For her unit on endangered species and extinction, Abigail Silver, of Washington, D.C., wants her 7th grade students to probe the complex ecological and human causes underlying extinction. At the same time, Abigail is also interested in teaching her students how to extract and interpret relative data from primary sources—a key skill in the new assessment tests. To these ends, Abigail is conducting a case-study lesson on the extinction of the passenger pigeon, using an adaptation of Such-

man's (1966) "Inquiry Strategy," known as "Mystery" (Silver et al., 1996). (For Abigail's analysis, see Figure 4.18.)

To introduce the lesson, Abigail sets up the mystery students will be asked to solve by explaining:

> In the mid-1800s, the passenger pigeon was so abundant in America that flocks measuring over 200 miles long were commonly reported. These flocks would sometimes blacken the sky for five hours at a time. The nesting area of a single flock could take up 1,000 square miles of forest. Sometimes, so many of these nine-ounce birds would occupy the trees in these forests that full-grown oaks would topple over from the weight.

> Yet by the late 1880s, finding a small flock of passenger pigeons was exceedingly difficult. By the turn of the century, there were only a few hundred left. Then in 1914, the last passenger pigeon died in an Ohio zoo. How is it possible that in only a few short years, the amount of passenger pigeons dwindled so drastically from legendary, almost mind-boggling abundance, to complete extinction?

Once Abigail has hooked the students into the mystery, she asks them to break up into small groups and to brainstorm some potential solutions to this puzzling situation. After discussing the results of the brainstorming session, Abigail explains to her students that each group will now have to develop a scientifically valid explanation for the disappearance of the passenger pigeon. In developing their solution, students examine and discuss a number of documents including newspaper articles, accounts of passenger pigeon hunts, advertisements, and pictures, which Abigail has collected from a book of primary documents relating to ecological disasters. During this period of analyzing documents, students collect and group relevant

FIGURE 4.18
ABIGAIL'S ANALYSIS OF THE MYSTERY STRATEGY

	MASTERY	UNDERSTANDING	SELF-EXPRESSIVE	INTERPERSONAL
V		Interpreting primary documents Evidence-based essay	Brainstorming	Group discussion Whole-class discussion
L		Collecting evidence	Formulating hypotheses	
S		Analyzing pictures		
M				
B				
P				Cooperative learning
I				
N	Background on extinction	Solving ecological mystery Collecting evidence		

Note: V = verbal-linguistic; L = logical-mathematical; S = spatial; M = musical; B = bodily- kinesthetic; P = interpersonal; I = intrapersonal; N = naturalist intelligence.

evidence that they believe helps explain the mystery. For instance, one student group organized its evidence into three groups and then converted its groupings into three hypotheses:

• Unlike the Native Americans, who had set hunting dates and places, European Americans hunted the pigeons all over the country and whenever the flocks appeared.

• Because the passenger pigeon relied on large flocks to survive, it was particularly vulnerable to extinction.

• All European Americans were to blame, not just the pigeon hunters.

To synthesize the lesson, Abigail conducts a discussion in which students talk about their learning, as well as the process of collecting evidence and solving scientific mysteries. Finally, students are required to write an ecologically sound, evidence-based explanation of how and why the passenger pigeon was pushed to extinction, along with recommendations about how to prevent further extinctions.

Designing the Instructional Unit: Teaching Around the Wheel

"Teaching Around the Wheel" is a systematic approach to designing and delivering integrated instructional units. In developing instructional units that integrate learning styles and multiple intelligences, you can use a simple, five-step planning template known as "IDEAS." This

FIGURE 4.19
SAMPLE STATEMENT: 3RD GRADE

Students will be able to use the following four punctuation marks correctly in their written communications: question mark, period, comma, and exclamation point.

process can flex to your needs and demands. If, for instance, you are more comfortable with learning styles than multiple intelligences, you might want to do Step 4, which deals with style integration, before you focus on intelligences (Steps 2 and 3). Do what feels comfortable— you know how you plan best.

Step 1: Identify the type of lesson you wish to teach and the specific standard(s), outcome(s), and objective(s), you want to address.

Completing the initial step requires that you ask yourself two questions:

1. Am I developing:
   • A lesson for using learning styles and multiple intelligences to achieve specific content objectives?
   • A lesson focused on the development of particular styles or intelligences?

2. Am I developing:
   • A lesson that's part of a year-long curricular theme?
   • A lesson to teach a specific objective?
   • A lesson to address a specific student need (i.e., for a student educational plan)?

Figures 4.19 and 4.20 show two different teachers' objectives.

FIGURE 4.20
SAMPLE STATEMENT: 8TH GRADE

Students will learn how to identify math problems that require use of the formula d (distance) $= r$ (rate) $\times t$ (time). Students will apply the formula to a variety of word problems.

Step 2: For each intelligence, develop a list of possible learning opportunities for students to achieve your objective(s).

To complete this step, you need to ask yourself a series of questions about how multiple intelligences can effectively be integrated into your lesson. Good questions include:

(**V**) How can I incorporate words, writing, listening, discussion, language?

(**L**) How can I incorporate calculation, problem solving, reasoning, math?

(**S**) How can I incorporate art, video, graphic organizers, icons, color?

(**B**) How can I incorporate manipulatives, hands-on learning, use of the body?

(**M**) How can I incorporate music, musicality, beat, lyrics, sound?

(**P**) How can I incorporate cooperative learning, partnerships, role-playing?

(**I**) How can I incorporate emotion, reflection, self-assessment?

(**N**) How can I incorporate interactions with the natural world?

Although it is not necessary to use all eight intelligences in every lesson, it is helpful to brainstorm activities in all of them. For now, list as many ideas as you can. Draw on the teaching strategies and activities you already use to see how they might fit in with the intelligences. If you are trying to focus on a particular intelligence or intelligences, then focus your brainstorming on those you want students to develop.

Step 3: Examine alternatives and select the most appropriate activities to achieve your learning goals.

From the ideas on your possibility list, select the approaches that seem most workable in your educational setting and that will enhance the effectiveness of the lesson (for a 3rd grade example, see Figure 4.21).

You might want to include some optional activities for certain students, and have extra activities for students who complete the work early.

Step 4: Assess what style activities or teaching strategies you can use to achieve your learning goals.

Next, you need to consider how you can incorporate style-based activities and strategies into your overall plan. To do this, refer to the thinking-verbs-by-style guide in Figure 4.22, which has been keyed to specific learning goals based on a simplified version of Bloom's Taxonomy of Education Objectives (1956).

Once you have selected your activities and strategies, place them into a style framework. Figure 4.23 (p. 68) shows the same 3rd-grade teacher's activity outline for incorporating all four learning styles into her lesson.

FIGURE 4.21
3RD GRADE INTELLIGENCE ACTIVITIES

Example of a 3rd grade teacher's intelligence activities for a punctuation unit.	
V	Explain uses of punctuation marks. Practice using each type in writing. Edit a text.
L	"Why do we need punctuation marks?" Classifying sentences.
S	Visual organizer. Icons and symbols. Collage about punctuation marks.
M	Rap song. Create jingles to represent marks.
B	Role play.
P	Group and peer practice, writers' clubs, edit partner's text.
I	Which is your favorite? Why? Personal narrative.
N	Natural similes (e.g., an exclamation point is like a lightning bolt because . . .)

Note: Intelligence abbreviations: V = verbal-linguistic; L = logical-mathematical; S = spatial; M = musical; B = bodily-kinesthetic; P = interpersonal; I = intrapersonal; N = naturalist.

FIGURE 4.22
THINKING VERBS BY STYLE AND OBJECTIVES

Goal	Mastery	Understanding	Self-Expressive	Interpersonal
Content acquisition	Examine Fact Find Gather Inspect Look-up Observe Recollect Review Scrutinize Seek	Ask Assess Inquire Investigate Probe Question Read Research Study	Anticipate Brainstorm Explore Generate Search Speculate	Elicit a response Feel Interview Listen Pursue Reflect Survey
Critical analysis	Assess Categorize Check Determine List Organize Prepare Sequence Take Notes Trace	Analyze Classify Compare Critique Deduce Evaluate Imply Infer Interpret Reason Resolve Weigh	Apply Combine Conceive Experiment Gauge Generalize Imagine Integrate Picture Predict Systematize	Appraise Appreciate Decide Deliberate Personalize Prioritize Rate Relate Value
Application of learning	Build Construct Depict Form Make Manufacture Solve	Advise Analyze Compose Develop Formulate Plan Prove Respond Write	Apply Create Design Draw Fabricate Frame Generate Invent Metaphorize Originate Paint Picture Produce	Coach Decide Editorialize Personify Role play Share
Dissemination and use of learning	Describe Display Demonstrate Inform Present Report Show	Convince Debate Disclose Explain Persuade Publish Teach Dialogue	Advertise Articulate Broadcast Communicate Disseminate Elaborate Elucidate Perform Produce Write	Advise Act Coach Convince Discuss Dialogue
Evaluation and improvement	Check Correct Reward Test	Assess Critique Evaluate Judge Weigh	Appreciate Amend Gauge Improve Respond Reflect	Appraise Approve Decide Evaluate React Value

FIGURE 4.23
3RD GRADE STYLE GRID

MASTERY ACTIVITIES	INTERPERSONAL ACTIVITIES
• Create a visual organizer to explain the uses of the four punctuation marks (V, L, S). • Correct a poorly punctuated text (V and L). • Have students practice punctuation using their bodies to represent the marks as the teacher reads sentences (B).	• Use *Team Games Tournament* to review use of punctuation marks (V, P). • *Reciprocal Learning:* Coaching each other (V, P). • *Writers Club* for editing, feedback on story (V, P). • Write a personal narrative using all learned punctuation marks (V, I).
• *Concept Attainment* (yes–no examples) for students to figure out which punctuation marks to use when (V, L). • *Inductive Learning:* Group and label sentences according to punctuation marks (V, L).	• Write a rap, jingle, or cinquain to explain when to use each punctuation mark (V, M). • Create a natural metaphor for each punctuation mark (e.g., a period is like a heavy rock) (V, S, N). • Draw a picture of the mark. Write a story and punctuate it (V, S, L).
UNDERSTANDING ACTIVITIES	**SELF-EXPRESSIVE ACTIVITIES**

Note: V = verbal-linguistic; L = logical-mathematical; S = spatial; M = musical; B = bodily-kinesthetic; P = interpersonal; I = intrapersonal; N = naturalist intelligence.

Step 5: Set up a sequential plan. Complete the Lesson Design Matrix.

Now you are ready to piece your work together. To do this, you will organize your unit onto a lesson design matrix. A Lesson Design Matrix is a simple, five-column tool that allows you to sequence your work into a seamless, meaningful whole. Figure 4.24 shows a completed Lesson Design Matrix for the lesson on punctuation.

This final step also entails figuring out the finishing details for your unit, including what materials will be needed, what an appropriate time frame would be, and any other details that need to be worked out before implementation.

FIGURE 4.24
LESSON DESIGN MATRIX

Purpose	Content	Process Activities-Strategies	Product	Interest: L.S.-M.I.
Learn the roles of punctuation marks	Natural metaphors	Metaphoric Expression, Kindling	Written explanation	• Self-expressive, Understanding • Verbal, spatial, naturalist
Learn when to use all four punctuation marks	Question mark, period, comma, exclamation point	Concept Attainment	Generate rules for using each type of punctuation	• Understanding • Verbal, logical
Explain punctuation rules	"	Visual Organizer	Completed organizer	• Mastery • Verbal, logical, spatial
Reinforce rules	"	Game	Play the game	• Mastery • Verbal, bodily
Practice using punctuation rules	Peer practice sheet—poorly punctuated text	Reciprocal Learning	Revised text	• Interpersonal, Mastery • Verbal, interpersonal
Apply skills	Question mark, period, comma, exclamation point	Write to Learn	Personal narrative	• Self-Expressive, Interpersonal, • Verbal, intrapersonal
"	Written narrative	Writers' club	Edited pieces	• Mastery, Understanding, Interpersonal • Verbal Intrapersonal

Note: L.S. = learning styles; M.I. = multiple intelligences.

Designing Integrated Performance Assessments

MULTIPLE INTELLIGENCES REPRESENT THE KINDS OF content students will find in the world. Learning styles embody the different ways people think as they learn, solve problems, and interact. Thus, it should come as little surprise that proponents of both models stress the need for assessment that emphasizes real-world applications and that favors realistic performances over out-of-context drill items. Howard Gardner (1997) argues for assessment practices that look "directly at the performance that we value, whether it's a linguistic, logical, aesthetic, or social performance" (pp. 12–13). Learning style expert Richard Strong (1999) similarly sees performance as central to probing students' understanding. He claims, "At the root of these assessments is performance. Such assessments require students to generate—rather than choose—a response, and to actively accomplish complex tasks while bringing to bear prior knowledge, new learning, and relevant skills" (Keynote at the 1999 National Conference on Standards and Assessment, Las Vegas, Nevada).

What Is Performance Assessment?

What if pilots could receive certification just by getting good grades on short-answer tests? Have you ever heard of a shortstop who could "knock 'em dead" on any written test on baseball, but didn't know how to swing a bat, field a grounder, or throw a ball? What if doctors never worked with patients during their training and learned about the nature, causes, and treatments of illness only by perusing medical textbooks? Surely, the expectation for members of vocations is that they can demonstrate their competence, that they will know how to perform well and complete tasks that are central to their chosen careers. Yet in many schools, assessment means asking students to take short-answer or multiple-choice tests that focus on monitoring students' factual knowledge, rather than on helping them better understand how their learning and their talents are applied in the world that awaits them. If we expect to assess students' understanding, then we need an assessment system that is driven by realistic problems and questions that make up the disciplines students learn and that asks students to engage in authentic and motivating work around these problems and questions. In the philosophy of performance assessment, to study biology is to think, act, and perform like a biologist—to conduct inquiries, test ideas, build

70

arguments, analyze data, and compare and contrast organisms—much more than it is to commit the types of protozoa to short-term memory for a test.

In general, we want students to discover their talents, abilities, and interests and to learn how to apply those talents in the world beyond the classroom. This then is the point of convergence between performance assessment, learning styles, and multiple intelligences: The fusion of styles and intelligences provides us with a comprehensive map of the varied ways students may express themselves and demonstrate their understanding of a topic. Integrated performance assessment means making the connections between styles, intelligence, and the real world explicit in a way that is useful to both students and teachers.

As you may remember from Chapter 3, in integrating learning styles and multiple intelligences, we moved through three steps:

• We divided each intelligence four ways, according to the four learning styles.

• We used vocational research and data to match careers to each style-intelligence profile.

• We used these vocations and teachers' assessments to develop a list of real-world assessment tasks that could be used in the classroom.

Out of this integration process came a set of assessment menus listing authentic performance-based tasks that can be used in any classroom and that revolve around style, intelligence, and real-world tasks. Figures 5.1 through 5.8 show these menus in detail. The menus make it easy for teachers to develop a style/intelligence-based assessment system that places a premium on forging authentic connections between school and the world outside school.

FIGURE 5.1
VERBAL-LINGUISTIC INTEGRATED ASSESSMENT MENU

• Write an article • Put together a magazine • Develop a plan • Develop a newscast • Describe a complex procedure/object	**MASTERY** The ability to use language to describe events and sequence activities *Journalist Technical Writer Administrator Contractor*	**INTERPERSONAL** The ability to use language to build trust and rapport *Salesperson Counselor Clergyperson Therapist*	• Write a letter • Make a pitch • Conduct an interview • Counsel a fictional character or a friend
	VERBAL-LINGUISTIC		
• Make a case • Make/defend a decision • Advance a theory • Interpret a text • Explain an artifact	The ability to develop logical arguments and use rhetoric *Lawyer Professor Orator Philosopher* **UNDERSTANDING**	The ability to use metaphoric and expressive language *Playwright Poet Novelist Advertising Copywriter* **SELF-EXPRESSIVE**	• Develop a plan to direct • Spin a tale • Develop an advertising campaign

FIGURE 5.2
LOGICAL-MATHEMATICAL INTEGRATED ASSESSMENT MENU

- Develop a budget
- Collect and analyze statistics
- Predict a trend

MASTERY

The ability to use numbers to compute, describe, and document

*Accountant   Bookkeeper
Statistician*

INTERPERSONAL

The ability to apply mathematics in personal and daily life

Tradesperson   Homemaker

- Weigh a decision
- Predict a trend
- Conduct a health survey
- Develop a household budget

LOGICAL-MATHEMATICAL

- Develop a formula
- Investigate an issue or problem
- Design a program
- Analyze a dilemma
- Write a chapter explaining a concept
- Create a matrix
- Conduct an experiment
- Debug a program

The ability to use mathematical concepts to conjecture, establish proofs, and apply mathematics and data to construct arguments

*Logician   Computer Programmer
Scientist Quantitative Problem Solver*

UNDERSTANDING

The ability to be sensitive to the patterns, symmetry, logic and aesthetics of mathematics and to solve problems in design and modeling

*Composer   Engineer Inventor
Designer   Qualitative Problem Solver*

SELF-EXPRESSIVE

- Create a game
- Draw up blueprints
- Produce a schedule
- Apply a concept to a real-life setting
- Explain an aesthetic trend in mathematical terms
- Write a "Hard Science" Sci-Fi Story

FIGURE 5.3
SPATIAL INTEGRATED ASSESSMENT MENU

- Create a map
- Develop a travel brochure
- Construct a flowchart

MASTERY

The ability to perceive and represent the visual-spatial world accurately

*Illustrator   Artist
Guide   Photographer*

INTERPERSONAL

The ability to arrange color, line, shape, form, and space to meet the needs of others

*Interior Decorator   Painter
Clothing Designer   Weaver
Builder*

- Create a set to fit a scene
- Develop a fashion line
- Design an addition to a home

SPATIAL

- Make a graph
- Create a chart
- Create an environment for specific needs
- Interpret trends from maps, graphs, charts
- Conduct a design analysis
- Interpret the significance of an image

The ability to interpret and graphically represent visual or spatial ideas

*Architect   Iconographer
Guide   Photographer*

UNDERSTANDING

The ability to transform visual or spatial ideas into imaginative and expressive creations

*Artist   Inventor
Model Builder   Cinematographer*

SELF-EXPRESSIVE

- Construct visually appealing graphs and charts
- Use visual art to express an opinion
- Create a cartoon strip
- Invent or design to solve a problem

FIGURE 5.4
BODILY-KINESTHETIC INTEGRATED ASSESSMENT MENU

- Develop an exercise or nutritional plan
- Construct from a plan
- Rebuild a complex structure

MASTERY

The ability to use the body and tools to take effective action or to construct or repair

*Mechanic   Trainer   Contractor
Craftsperson   Tool and Dye Maker*

INTERPERSONAL

The ability to use the body to build rapport, to console and/or persuade, and to support others

*Coach   Counselor
Salesperson   Trainer*

- Present a motivational speech
- Create a tableau
- Develop a plan for individual therapy
- Analyze body language

BODILY-KINESTHETIC

- Analyze health and fitness data
- Compare and contrast healthy and unhealthy lifestyles
- Choreograph a concept
- Teach a physical education concept
- Critique others' positions on health

The ability to plan strategically or to critique the actions of the body

*Physical Educator   Sports Analyst
Professional Athlete   Dance Critic*

UNDERSTANDING

The ability to appreciate the aesthetics of the body and to use those values to create new forms of expression.

*Sculptor   Choreographer
Actor Dancer   Mime Puppeteer*

SELF-EXPRESSIVE

- Create a diorama or display
- Represent ideas in dance/drama
- Act out emotional states or concepts
- Develop a plan for directing a scene

FIGURE 5.5
MUSICAL INTEGRATED ASSESSMENT MENU

- Create an audio tape using real-life sounds to illustrate a concept
- Analyze the structure of a symphony
- Analyze or create a musical instrument

MASTERY

The ability to understand and develop musical technique

*Technician   Music Teacher
Instrument Maker*

INTERPERSONAL

The ability to respond emotionally to music and to work together to use music to meet the needs of others

*Choral, Band, and Orchestral
Performer and/or Conductor
Public Relations in Music*

- Perform a piece of music that will help others understand a concept.
- Design an album cover
- Design an advertising plan using music

MUSICAL

- Analyze the meaning, significance, and causes of changes in music
- Compare and contrast music from different cultures or times
- Use rhythm to reinforce or illustrate a concept

The ability to interpret musical forms and ideas

*Music Critic   Aficionado
Music Collector*

UNDERSTANDING

The ability to create imaginative and expressive performances and compositions

*Composer   Conductor
Individual/Small Group Performer*

SELF-EXPRESSIVE

- Create a rap, song, jingle, sonata, etc.
- Select music for key scenes in a play, novel, or poem
- Put together a musical program

FIGURE 5.6
INTERPERSONAL INTEGRATED ASSESSMENT MENU

- Develop a plan to solve a social problem
- Investigate an issue and report your findings

MASTERY

The ability to organize people and to communicate clearly what needs to be done

*Administrator   Manager
Politician*

INTERPERSONAL

The ability to use empathy to help others and to solve problems

*Social Worker   Doctor   Nurse
Therapist   Teacher*

- Develop a correspondence with real, historical, or fictional characters
- Assess group functioning
- Teach a concept to a younger student

INTERPERSONAL

- Conduct a psychological analysis of a fictional or historical character
- Argue fairy tales are psychologically sound or unsound
- Apply psychological or sociological concepts to history or literature

The ability to discriminate and interpret among different kinds of interpersonal clues

*Sociologist   Psychologist
Psychotherapist
Professor (Psychology, Sociology)*

UNDERSTANDING

The ability to influence and inspire others to work towards a common goal

*Consultant   Charismatic Leader
Politician   Evangelist*

SELF-EXPRESSIVE

- Write a speech or sermon
- Develop a plan for resolving an interpersonal or sociological dilemma
- Defend a cause

FIGURE 5.7
INTRAPERSONAL INTEGRATED ASSESSMENT MENU

- Design a business proposal that takes your own qualifications as an owner into consideration
- Develop a set of plans and then connect them to school life
- Create a budget to solve a personal problem

MASTERY

The ability to assess one's own strengths, weaknesses, talents, and interests and to use them to set goals

Planner   Small Business Owner

INTERPERSONAL

The ability to use understanding of oneself to be of service to others

Counselor   Social Worker

- Observe and keep a diary on someone you know or have studied
- Develop a plan for aiding a character from history or literature
- Interview someone about a meaningful issue

INTRAPERSONAL

- Investigate people's responses to issues, characters, works of art, etc.
- Investigate your own responses and look for patterns

The ability to form and develop concepts and theories based on an examination of oneself

Psychologist

UNDERSTANDING

The ability to reflect upon one's inner moods, intuitions, and temperament and to use them to create or express a personal vision

Artist   Religious Leader   Writer

SELF-EXPRESSIVE

- Write a sermon based on a concept
- Create a work of art that illustrates your perspective on an issue
- Write an autobiography
- Find connections between your own life and what you learn in school

FIGURE 5.8
NATURALIST INTEGRATED ASSESSMENT MENU

- Study a natural issue and report your findings
- Care for a plant or animal
- Write a biography of a famous naturalist
- Describe a natural object accurately

MASTERY

The ability to work with nature directly and effectively

Farmer   Gardener   Ranger
Horticulturist   Zoologist

INTERPERSONAL

The ability to use and harness nature to help others and improve people's lives

Chef   Pharmacist   Doctor
Holistic Medicine   Veterinarian

- Develop a nutritional plan for your family
- Teach a natural concept to a younger student
- Write a poem or play about how nature helps people

NATURALIST

- Investigate and develop a solution for an environmental problem
- Conduct an experiment
- Argue for an environmental cause
- Develop a taxonomy for plants, animals, or natural objects

The ability to analyze/classify natural objects and develop strategies for solving ecological problems

Biologist   Meteorologist
Ecologist   Environmental Lawyer

UNDERSTANDING

The ability to appreciate and express the aesthetic qualities of nature

Landscape Designer   Florist
Nature Photographer/Artist

SELF-EXPRESSIVE

- Beautify your school-yard
- Imagine a "natureless" society. Describe how people would be affected
- Create a nature-based photo journal

Using Integrated Assessment Menus

To facilitate the implementation of this assessment system in the classroom, keep the following guidelines in mind when using the Integrated Assessment Menus:

1. The menus should be used as a compass. This means that in using these menus, you should keep track of what styles and intelligences you are emphasizing, as well as those you may be avoiding. In this way, you can bring balance and equity to your assessment system. In addition, you can note how students respond to different style–intelligence assessments and help them search for different choices when particular assessments don't work for them.

One teacher made a grid of her unit plans and identified the styles and intelligences each activity/assessment emphasized. She continued using this format for all her unit planning and was consequently able to see how her teaching and assessment practices were reaching out to all styles and intelligences. Figure 5.9 shows a sample grid.

2. Start simply and progress as you feel comfortable. For simplicity's sake, you might begin by focusing on only one intelligence at a time. In this way, you are working with only one menu at a time. Then you can focus on the stylistic element of the intelligence. For instance, you might allow students to choose the style they wish to work in or allow them to work in one style they like, as well as one they would normally avoid, to both challenge and accommodate them. Figure 5.10 (p. 78) shows a sample assessment designed by Carl Carrozza of Catskill, New York, which focuses on bodily-kinesthetic intelligence in all four styles:

FIGURE 5.9
INVENTIONS

Activity	Style	Intelligence	
Analyze Inventions Select an item from the invention box below. Form a team of students and brainstorm ideas on how your item might have been invented. When the group comes to an agreement about how the item was invented, the team should make a presentation to the class. Then, research the actual invention of the selected item. Compare your group's ideas with the actual process. Present your findings in a report. pizza　　hair dryer　　telephone bicycle　　diaper　　adhesive tape	ST___ SF___ NT___ NF___	V___　　B___ L___　　P___ S___　　I___ M___　　N___	
Problem-Solving Identify a list of problems that may need an invention. Select one and brainstorm ideas on how it could be solved. Use your Divergent Thinking strategy to come up with different ideas. Construct your invention or a model, and test it to see if it will work to solve the problem.	ST___ SF___ NT___ NF___	V___　　B___ L___　　P___ S___　　I___ M___　　N___	

Style abbreviations: ST = sensing-thinking (Mastery); SF = sensing-feeling (Interpersonal); NT = intuitive-thinking (Understanding); NF = intuitive-feeling (Self-Expressive) learner. *Intelligence abbreviations:* V = verbal-linguistic; L = logical-mathematical; S = spatial; B = bodily-kinesthetic; M = musical; P = interpersonal; I = intrapersonal; N = naturalist.

FIGURE 5.9 CONTINUED

Activity	Style		Intelligence	
Reflection Record your thoughts and work notes on your invention. Include diagrams, notes to yourself, and conversations with others.	ST___ SF___ NT___ NF___		V___ L___ S___ M___	B___ P___ I___ N___
Selling Your Ideas Make an advertisement for your invention. It can be a poster, a magazine ad, radio ad, or a videotape "infomercial." In your ad, explain how your invention works and what its benefits to the public are.	ST___ SF___ NT___ NF___		V___ L___ S___ M___	B___ P___ I___ N___
How to Patent an Invention Collect information on how an invention is patented. Develop a flow chart showing the process.	ST___ SF___ NT___ NF___		V___ L___ S___ M___	B___ P___ I___ N___
Definitions Define these terms: *trademark* and *copyright*. Create a visual icon for each idea. Explain how the ideas are similar to a patent and how they are different from a patent.	ST___ SF___ NT___ NF___		V___ L___ S___ M___	B___ P___ I___ N___
"Thomas Edison Day" As a way to celebrate all of our work, we will have a "Thomas Edison Day" in which all inventions, advertisements, patents, drawings, inventor's logs, and research are displayed for parents, teachers, and students to enjoy.	ST___ SF___ NT___ NF___		V___ L___ S___ M___	B___ P___ I___ N___

FIGURE 5.10
SINGLE INTELLIGENCE TASK ROTATION

MASTERY

List as many sports as you can where the athlete remains aerobic the whole time.

List as many sports as you can where the athlete is often in an anaerobic state.

UNDERSTANDING

To be a successful athlete, you must duplicate the performance desired from your body in competition during practice. Design a conditioning workout for basketball players. Demonstrate the workout to your classmates.

INTERPERSONAL

If you open and close your hand quickly, over and over, you will feel a "burn" in your hand and forearm as the muscles build up lactic acid. If you slow down, the discomfort goes away. With a partner, determine the fastest rate you can open and close your hand before the "burn" occurs. Determine how many hand closures for each minute that is. This rate is the anaerobic threshold of your hand.

SELF-EXPRESSIVE

Invent a new sport. Describe the object of the game, tell about its important features, and, most importantly, describe the aerobic and anaerobic demands the sport would have on the athlete. Demonstrate one or two moves from your sport.

Source: Carl Carrozza of Catskill, New York. Adapted by permission.

Over time, you may choose to mix styles and intelligences. Figure 5.11, for instance, shows a culminating assessment developed by 1st grade teacher Charlene Larkin of Whitney Point Central, New York, for a unit on plants. Notice how she has mixed styles and intelligences so that students are being asked to use and develop a wide range of abilities.

You can also add levels of achievement to create a comprehensive assessment menu from which students may select the task or tasks they wish to complete (see Figure 5.12). The advantage of this approach is that it provides greater opportunities for each student to succeed by selecting her own appropriate level of performance. It also allows teachers to work more effectively with students of differing abilities. After students have completed their work, they should be encouraged to reflect on their choice and their performance and to develop a set of goals for achieving at a higher level next time. Quality teacher feedback, which is essential to

FIGURE 5.11
MIXED INTELLIGENCE TASK ROTATION

Task Rotation
Plant Unit
Kindergarten/1st Grade

For each question, students draw, write, and explain their responses.

Mastery Style

Draw a flowering plant and label its parts.

(Spatial Intelligence)

Interpersonal Style

How would you feel on a sunny (or rainy) day if you were a plant?

(Intrapersonal Intelligence)

Understanding Style

Why are plants important to our world? Think of two reasons.

(Logical-Mathematical Intelligence)

Self-Expressive Style

What would our world look like if there were no plants? Describe it.

(Verbal-Linguistic and Spatial Intelligences)

Source: Charlene Larkin, Whitney Point Central, New York. Adapted by permission.

any assessment process, is especially important in this case. Teachers can set up conferences to discuss student choice, comfort levels, and performance.

3. Think of the menus as a map of all your students' interests and potential. The menus provide students with dozens of methods for demonstrating what they know. Allow students to become familiar with the menus and find their own interests in them. For instance, when doing research or creative projects, show students the menus and let them select their own approach to expressing their knowledge of a topic.

FIGURE 5.12
WAR MENU: CAUSES OF WAR IN THE 20TH CENTURY

1

Where and When
Locate, on a set of world maps, where major conflicts for each decade in the 20th century occurred and construct a visual time line.

Examining Data
Examine the causes of the following conflicts:
- World War I (WWI)
- World War II (WWII)
- Korean War
- Vietnam War

List and group them. Convert you analysis into a visual organizer explaining the fundamental causes of war.

Metaphorical Expression
War has been compared to the eruption of a volcano. Generate a list of five other things war can be compared to. Select one and create a visual poster to explain how the causes of a particular conflict in the 20th century was like the idea you selected.

Interpersonal Conflicts
Interview three people about personal conflicts they have had. Based on your interview, what do you feel are the causes for such conflicts? Speculate whether these causes are similar to nations going to war.

2

What Is the Cause?
Select two major conflicts, each from a different decade and research them. Identify who was involved in the conflict, what were the causes of the conflict, how the conflict was resolved, and the implications of the resolution for the future.

Support or Refute
It has been said that "war in the 20th century was inevitable" due to the growth of nationalism, economic competition, materialism, the birth of democracy, and the competition for diminishing resources. What evidence do you have to support or refute this premise? Prepare a newspaper editorial expressing your position and why.

What If . . .
Select one of the following hypothetical events and speculate how history would be different politically, socially, geographically, and economically in the 20th century if it were to occur. Explain your reasoning.
- If the treaty of Versailles treated Germany equally.
- If the United States had joined the League of Nations at the end of WWI.
- If the Soviet Union and the United States remained allies after WWII instead of engaging in a cold war.
- If the United States refrained from the use of nuclear weapons to end WWII against Japan.
- If the military industrial complex had been dismantled at the end of the Korean War as President Eisenhower suggested.

Arousing Feelings
No one wants to go to war. However, leaders have influenced their constituents to support their nation's involvement. Select two conflicts and research how emotions and feelings were manipulated to support going to war.

FIGURE 5.12 CONTINUED

| 3 | **Where Next?** Prepare a briefing for the Armed Services Commission identifying three areas of potential conflict for the future. Identify who might be involved in the conflict, what might be the causes, and what actions might be available to the United States to prevent or ease the tensions in this area. Use visuals, graphs, and mathematics to support your presentation. | **What Have We Learned?** Based on your study of conflict in the 20th century, what have you learned about the causes of such conflict and how they might be prevented? Prepare a 3–5 minute speech to be given to world leaders at the United Nations. Include the advice you would give to these leaders to make the world safe from war in the 21st century. Use visuals, graphs, and mathematics to support your presentation. | **Creative Product** It is said that music and art are expressions of our times. Based on your analysis of the causes of war, create one of the following:
• Construct a collage of the causes of war.
• Write a selection of poetry on the causes of war.
• Write a one-act play or write a musical composition on the causes of war and perform it for the class.
• Prepare a diary which tells how you went about creating your product. Tell about the problems you faced and how you resolved them. Discuss your position, your analysis, and your method to communicate it. | **What Would You Do?** Read about the Vietnam antiwar movement. Prepare a scrapbook of the times that tells about it. Interview two people who fought in the war and two who did not. Depict the position of the antiwar movement, the techniques they used to protest the war, and the effect they had on the war. Use the scrapbook to express your position on the war. Also, give your opinion on what constitutes a just cause to start a war or why there is no justification for war. |

When allowing students to design their own tasks, it is a good idea to provide them with a simple assessment-design worksheet (like the one in Figure 5.13 (p. 83), which has been completed by a student) so that they see what a quality task contains as they develop one. Confer with students about their task ideas.

4. Assess your assessment to keep it thoughtful. Be critical of your assessments. Before they reach your students, evaluate how well they meet instructional purposes. Use the following simple rubric:

Content

Thoughtful performance assessments are based on challenging and meaningful content necessary for students' full development as learners, as citizens, and as workers.

| 0 | 1 | 2 | 3 | 4 |

Thought

Thoughtful performance assessments require complex, nonroutine thinking, rather than mere recall of factual information or the demonstration of routine repetitive skills.

| 0 | 1 | 2 | 3 | 4 |

Products and Performance

Thoughtful performance assessments provide students with opportunities to create significant products and performances (as opposed to short answers) that are extended to reveal students' thought processes and individual methods or approaches.

| 0 · | 1 | 2 | 3 | 4 |

Authenticity and Interest

Thoughtful performance assessments create strong connections between real world contexts, student interests, and opportunities to apply knowledge in meaningful ways.

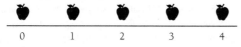

| 0 | 1 | 2 | 3 | 4 |

A Warning. No performance assessment, no matter how thoughtful and skilled its creator, can reach the highest level of achievement on all these scales. There will always be trade-offs, one standard against another, and all standards against the realities of our time, our energy, our resources, and the political and community realities that affect all our teaching decisions. Still, we hope that by making the standards of thoughtful assessment clear, we can clarify the directions in which we are trying to evolve.

Learning Styles, Multiple Intelligences, and "A Test Worth Taking"

Integrated assessment is not only about student performance, and it is not an attempt to force traditional assessment out of our schools. Instead, integrated assessment should be focused on bringing a healthy balance to our assessment practices so that we are able to assess students deeply through performance and also to obtain a breadth of information about each learner's skills

and content knowledge. Obtaining a breadth of information brings us to what has become something of a dirty word in the language of performance assessment: *testing*. Not all tests, however, need to be the kinds of decontextualized auditing of factual knowledge that proponents of performance have rightly criticized.

In their recent work on developing tests designed around learning styles, multiple intelligences, and motivational research, Claudia Geocaris and Maria Ross (1999) define what they call "A Test Worth Taking." Figure 5.14 (p. 84) shows the principles that drive such a test, along with relevant sample test items. As you look this information over, note how Geocaris and Ross's test differs from a traditional test. How are these changes beneficial?

Clearly a test need not, and should not, mean a time when learning ceases and students are audited for their factual knowledge through fill-in-the-blank, multiple-choice, and short-answer items. Instead, as Geocaris and Ross report, this improved test—which students take over a two-day period—forces students to actively determine and fill in the gaps in their knowledge base as they choose the items they need to complete to receive 100 points.

The result of this is a test that respects students' styles and intelligences, that allows them to choose the ways in which they can best demonstrate their understanding, that requires them to think critically and seek out new knowledge, and that continues—rather than audits—the learning process. Like a traditional test, "a test worth taking" provides teachers with a broad picture of students' understanding, but it goes much further by including a section that generates useful feedback for both the teacher and student and by building in time for metacognitive and reflective thinking (itself a wonderful engagement of intrapersonal intelligence). Unlike traditional testing practices, "a test worth taking" asks students to consider

FIGURE 5.13
ASSESSMENT DESIGN WORKSHEET

Every learning task contains . . .

A Content Focus

My task will focus on: the causes of the Dust Bowl and how feelings get preserved.

At Least One Style of Thought (Learning Style)

Self-Expressive: Pretend I'm in the Dust Bowl. Create a product that reflects how I feel.
Interpersonal: Try to identify with the feelings of people in history.

At Least One Intelligence

Musical: Write a folk song.
Interpersonal: Perform it for the class.
Verbal-Linguistic: Study lyrics to songs by Arlo Guthrie and Bob Dylan to find out what folk lyrics sound like.

Description of Task

I am going to write and sing a folk song that explains what people went through during the Dust Bowl. It is the heart of the Dust Bowl. The crops are gone, so there's not much to do but worry. I'm going to write a song about what I am going through. I want to save my feelings for future generations so that they know what happened, why it happened, and how it has affected me.

how well they performed and, more important, how they might do better next time.

A test like this one has many benefits. According to Geocaris and Ross (1999), student responses were overwhelmingly positive. Some students even asked when the next test would be because they felt so empowered by the freedom they were given to use their various styles and intelligences to complete tasks of their choice. Among the few students who preferred traditional tests, the common reasoning was that multiple-choice questions allowed them to guess at answers even if they had no understanding of the content whatsoever. From the teachers' point of view, the test proved equally exciting:

> As students took the test, they read and reviewed introductory paragraphs of key concepts. They applied the information from one part of the test to assist them on another section. But most important, they were challenged to make choices that would allow them to express themselves in a style that matched their own (p. 32).

FIGURE 5.14

A TEST WORTH TAKING: CELL TEST

Principle	Sample Test Item
The test should begin with a purpose that connects previous knowledge and previews topics yet to be covered.	Understanding cell structure and function is essential to understanding biology. This knowledge helps us understand why organisms behave as they do, how they develop and reproduce, and how they are affected by environmental factors. The knowledge that you have gained in this unit will be the foundation for our studies in genetics and evolution.
The tests should be written as a narrative.	Every individual cell exists in a liquid environment. Even the cells of multicellular organisms, such as a maple tree or a human, are bathed in liquid. That is why we say that the human body is made up of mostly water. The presence of a liquid environment makes it easier for such materials as food, oxygen, and water to move into and out of the cell. There are several ways in which materials enter and leave the cell. Two such processes are diffusion and osmosis. In the next section of the test, you will have an opportunity to show me what you have learned about these two processes.
The test should have a section for students to explain in their own words what they have learned in the unit.	Take five minutes to tell me everything you think is important to know about the cell—its parts and their functions.
The test should provide choice.	Complete A or B A. What are the differences among cells, organs, tissues, and systems? Use a chart to record your answers. B. Describe the relationship among cells, organs, tissues, and systems to a 10-year-old by using words and pictures.
The test should involve all four learning styles and as many multiple intelligences as appropriate.	Compare and contrast active and passive transport. How are they different? How are they similar? Correctly match the parts of the cell with their functions. Using the materials available, prepare two slides—one of an animal cell and one of a plant cell. Show me your slides before you place them under a microscope. I will then watch you place the slide under the microscope and correctly locate and focus the image. Finally, make a drawing of what you see and label the parts of the cells. Scientists often use metaphors to describe scientific phenomena. Create a metaphor that accurately explains the relationship of the parts of the cell to their functions.
The test should provide clear directions and emphasize competency rather than grades.	Your goal in taking this test is to earn 100 points. It is not necessary to answer all the questions on the test. For each section, you will need to select the question(s) that you feel most comfortable answering. Remember to answer the questions completely. Do not rush through the test! This is your chance to choose the questions that will give you the best opportunity to show me what you have learned in the unit.
The test should be interesting and provide feedback for both the students and the teacher.	How well did the activities that we did in class help you prepare for this test? How much time did you spend preparing for this test?
The test should have a section for student reflection.	How do you feel about the way this test was written? What else do you know about the cell that was not asked on this test?

Source: Geocaris, C., & Ross, M. (1999, September). A test worth taking. *Educational Leadership, 57*(1), 29–33. Adapted by permission.

6 Teaching Learning Styles and Multiple Intelligences to Students

MANY TEACHERS WHO USE LEARNING STYLES AND multiple intelligences in their classrooms wonder how important it is for students to know about these models. Experience has taught us that students who understand the models are better able to understand their own learning profiles, to develop flexibility and adaptability in their thinking, and to set realistic goals about minimizing learning weaknesses and maximizing strengths. In fact, research on the importance of metacognitive thinking supports the notion that instructional approaches that help students reflect on their own learning processes are highly beneficial to their overall learning and tend to stimulate motivation to improve as learners (Brown, 1989; Marzano et al., 1988).

When students engage in this kind of "thinking about thinking," they become more self-directed and are able to select appropriate strategies for particular learning situations. In Libertyville, Illinois, where high schoolers take a course in style-based metacognition, course instructor Sue Ulrey explains, "We want students to understand what sorts of learning styles there are and how to interpret their own behavior in

learning. This leads to greater self-awareness." (Caccamo, 1998, Section 5, p. 3) Because models of learning can be taught rather easily to children as young as 1st grade (Armstrong, 1994), many teachers teach students about learning style and multiple intelligences so they can better understand themselves as students and as people. Of course, students—and teachers—must understand that styles and intelligences are not simply categories of identification; any description of a learner is an approximation. Both models are useful ways of helping us to understand our own strengths and weaknesses as learners so that we may grow and become more balanced. This chapter will show you a compendium of methods some teachers use to teach both models to their students..

Teaching Students About Learning Styles

Demonstration

Barb Heinzman of Geneva, New York, led her students through the following hands-on "Apple" demonstration to teach them about perception and judgment:

"Apple" Demo

Everyone uses four ways to learn. Today we will learn how we use our four functions to learn about an apple. [Barb has apples in a bag, one for each student in a group.]

One way to learn about something is through your five senses: your eyes, ears, nose, touch, and taste. Your senses tell you what something looks like, tastes like, feels like, and so forth. Select an apple and use your senses to describe your apple.

Another way to learn about something is to use your sixth sense. This is called intuition. It helps you to learn about things that you can't see, touch, taste, or smell. It helps you to make guesses or to use your imagination. Imagine what your apple might taste like or imagine where it comes from. Intuition also helps you to symbolize things. What are some things your apple might symbolize? Some examples might be good health or New York City. Use your intuition to come up with a new idea of what an apple might symbolize.

Still another way to learn about an apple is to use your thinking. Your thinking helps you to understand the purpose for things. For example, thinking helps you to understand the parts of an apple and what their functions are. Identify some of the parts of your apple—stem, skin, seed, pulp—and think about what each part does.

The last way to learn about something is to use your feelings. Feelings tell you if you like or dislike something. Do you feel you will like your apple? Discuss what you like or dislike about it.

Now, put your apple back in the bag. With your eyes closed, try to find your apple using all of your senses.

Questioning in Style

Another way to teach students about the four learning styles is to have them experience activities or questions in each of the four styles and then ask them to reflect on the thinking they used to answer the question or complete the activities.

For example, after reading a story, Barb Heinzman asks her students questions about what they remember (Mastery), questions that require explaining and proving (Understanding), questions that require the use of their imagination (Self-Expressive), or questions that invite students to reflect on and share their feelings (Interpersonal). Barb used the questions in Figure 6.1 to help students comprehend and hook into the first chapter of the historical novel *My Brother Sam Is Dead*.

FIGURE 6.1
QUESTIONS IN STYLE—*MY BROTHER SAM IS DEAD*

What is happening in the story? Who are the characters and what are their traits?	Which character do you relate to the most? The father, Sam, or Tim? Whom do you agree with, Sam or his father?
What is the meaning of the story? Why are the characters arguing?	What do you imagine Tim is thinking during this argument? How is a colony like a child?

Note: See Collier, J. L., & Collier, C. (1989). *My brother Sam is dead*. New York: Scholastic Paperbacks.

Barb reinforced that the Mastery style focuses on remembering; Understanding style, on reasoning or explaining; the Self-Expressive style, on imagining or creating; and the Interpersonal style, on relating or feelings. She then asked her students to stop after answering each question and to think about which type of thinking they used. By the end of the day the students understood the four learning styles. Next, she asked her students to pay attention to which styles of thinking they enjoyed the most; which they found difficult to do; and which they wanted to get better at. Soon the students were able to analyze activities and diagnose their own learning styles and profiles.

Of course, four-style questioning can be used at any grade level. With primary students, it is important to use words that are easy to understand. A 1st grade teacher made her presentation on styles particularly memorable by using a visual organizer of a face and by using simplified words, rather than abstract style categories (see Figure 6.2).

FIGURE 6.2
HEAD ORGANIZER

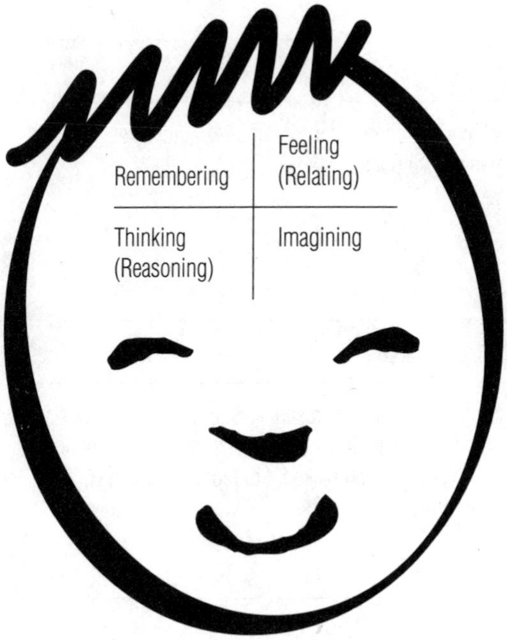

Similarly, four-style questioning is also effective with secondary students. Figure 6.3 shows an activity a high school English teacher used in conjunction with Robert Frost's poem "The Road Not Taken" to help her students become more aware of style, as well as better readers of poetry.

FIGURE 6.3
QUESTIONS IN STYLE—SECONDARY LEVEL:
POEM "THE ROAD NOT TAKEN"

What is happening in the poem? Who is speaking? Identify the rhyme scheme.	Do you relate to this poem? Tell about a hard decision you have made.
What is the meaning of the poem? What is meant by "And that has made all the difference?"	What do you imagine the poet was thinking when he wrote this? How is a decision like a fork in the road?

Or, rather than developing questions in style, you may assign students tasks in style. This method asks students to complete four tasks while simultaneously reflecting on their style preferences and dislikes. One particularly effective way to use tasks in style is to assign tasks that have to do with learning styles as *content*. This way, students are deepening their own understanding of learning styles while they are becoming more aware of who they are as learners. Figures 6.4 and 6.5 provide elementary and secondary examples, respectively, of tasks in various learning styles.

FIGURE 6.4
TASKS IN STYLE—ELEMENTARY

Mastery **Make a List**	**Relating** **The Helping Hand**
1. Write your name on four pieces of paper. 2. Write the name of one learning style on the top of each page. 3. Trace the correct icon on the bottom of each page. 4. List three facts about each learning style on the four pages.	Trace your hand. In each finger, write or draw something that tells a friend about yourself as a learner.
Understanding **Explain**	**Self-Expressive** **Picture This**
Compare your learning style to that of a classmate or relative. Include the strengths and weaknesses of the two styles you are comparing.	Pick four animals to represent each of the learning styles. On separate pieces of drawing paper, draw and color each animal. Then explain why you picked it to represent a particular learning style.

FIGURE 6.5
TASKS IN STYLE—SECONDARY

Mastery	**Relating**
Write the name of each learning style. Under the name, write three facts about that learning style. Then, pick a character who represents that style.	Develop a lesson plan for teaching learning styles to an elementary school student.
Understanding	**Self-Expressive**
Write a brief essay that compares your learning style to that of a classmate or relative. Include the strengths and weaknesses of the two styles you are comparing.	Pick four symbols to represent each of the learning styles. On separate pieces of drawing paper, draw each symbol. Then explain why you picked it to represent a particular learning style.

Reflecting in Style

Similar to questioning in style, reflecting in style asks students to think back on work they have done and to use the four styles to develop a deep awareness of how they think and work (see Figure 6.6). The goal of this task is to determine how the lessons learned about the self might be applied to the next project.

Descriptions and Case Studies

Another method is to have students read descriptions about the four styles and to think about which style sounds most like them and which sounds least like them. Stacey Gerhardt of Geneva, New York, gives her students case studies that sound like the one shown in Figure 6.7.

FIGURE 6.6
REFLECTING IN STYLE

What did you do to complete the project? Describe the steps you took.

What did you like about doing this project?

What didn't you like?

How has carrying out this project changed the way you view yourself as a learner?

Which steps worked best for you? Why do you think so?

As you did the project, what didn't work so well for you?

How do you know you did a good job?

How do you know the project was done well? List at least three reasons.

In doing this project, what did you learn that you might apply in doing another project?

In doing the project, what did you learn?

If you were to do this project again, what might you do differently?

The following four passages were written by four different 5th and 6th grade students about their experiences at school. Each student represents one of the four learning styles: Each is either a Mastery, Interpersonal, Understanding, or Self-Expressive learner. Read the passages and decide which one sounds the most like you. Underline any words or phrases that describe behaviors you can identify with.

The Cast of Characters

Samuel T.: Mastery Learner
I will often make a list of my next day's activities so I can be ready. Then I can check them off when I get them done, which usually happens. I don't mind class projects, as long as the teacher gives us an exact set of directions as to what is due and when. Usually I turn in those projects a few days early to make sure I have them done. Teachers like my work, although they say that I need to be more flexible and realize that there isn't always a right and a wrong answer. I am not *exactly* sure what they mean by that. I come to school to learn, and so I like it when the teacher shows me exactly what to do and what the answers are. I know I have mastered the material when I get a test or project back and everything on it is 100 percent right.

Nina F.: Self-Expressive Learner
Other kids usually like to have me on their project team because I always have lots of ideas. I like it best when the teacher says, "You pick a project and create what you want." Don't you think that's what school should be for? I mean, it should be a place where they let you come and explore ideas instead of page after page of stuff! I really like thinking of things to do, although all of my "brainy ideas" don't always come off. Of course, the more ideas we can come up with, and the crazier they are, the better for me. I sometimes get into trouble because I finish assignments at the last minute. I don't really forget them, it's just that some of the routine junk really bores me. Sometimes I'll get so involved in an idea that's not necessarily the one we're working on, I forget about the one I have to turn in!

Nancy T.: Understanding Learner
I like learning about ideas and their history and the reasons that people believe in them. The part of a class that I like best is when we get a chance to really think through a topic, usually on paper but sometimes out loud in discussion. I remember my mom saying that as a little kid I was always asking "Why?" I guess that hasn't changed much. If people give me a chance to compare choices and make my own decisions, I usually make the right one. I think school is a great place to find out all sorts of things. If, after a long discussion or an assignment, I have been able to look at all the different viewpoints and

FIGURE 6.7 CONTINUED

start to understand them, then I feel like I haven't wasted my time. For this reason, I guess I like essay tests the best because they give me some time to really express my opinions and prove my ideas.

Shamir F.: Interpersonal Learner

You might call me a "people person." It always makes me feel good to know that I have helped someone, even if it's just talking something over. Now that I think about it, I have always been the one moved by the teacher because I talk so much in class. That never bothered me so much because then I got to meet new people! I wasn't trying to go against the teacher. It's just that I find it more interesting doing work with a friend or a group than by myself. That's the best thing about school—lots of action among friends. People have told me that I get too "emotionally involved" with everything, but I really like finding out how others feel about things and what they are doing about them. I am happiest when the teacher divides us into groups to develop some project together, and I really get into an assignment when it relates somehow to me.

Rank the four characters according to their similarity to you:

1. **Not at all like me; 2. A little like me; 3. Somewhat like me; or 4. A lot like me.**

Samuel T.	Nina F.	Nancy T.	Shamir F.

How can you explain this order? Does it tell you anything about yourself?

Descriptions at the high school level look different from those in Figure 6.7. For example, Figure 6.8 provides a sample description a high school teacher developed for both styles and intelligences. Students then had to identify and explain how they knew what style (and intelligences) they exemplified.

Checklists and Inventories

Checklists and inventories are valuable tools that help students reflect on their preferred behaviors. Simple checklists are sufficient for primary and lower elementary students. For example, 3rd grade teacher Joanne Curran of Ladue Schools, Missouri, introduces and uses the checklist shown in Figure 6.9, with the following directions:

We are all able to learn in different ways. But just like you have a favorite toy or TV show, you also have a favorite style of learning. Because of your learning style, there are things that you really enjoy. There are other things that you may not like at all. No style is better than another.

They are just different. Sometimes, we need to be able to work in a style that is not our favorite because it's the best way to get a job done.

Finding out your favorite learning style is as simple as 1–2–3:
1. Color in the circle next to any sentences that seem to fit you.
2. Count the number of circles you colored in each square.
3. Circle the box with the most colored-in circles. It is probably your favorite learning style.

At upper elementary through secondary levels, the best means for identifying and helping students reflect on their strengths and weaknesses as learners is to use the Hanson-Silver *Learning Preference Inventory* (LPI) (1991), currently used in hundreds of schools across the United States. The LPI contains 36 multiple-choice questions whose answers are keyed to each of the four learning styles (as well as to tendencies for introversion and extroversion). Figure 6.10 shows some examples of LPI items.

FIGURE 6.8
HIGH SCHOOL CASE STUDY

Brad: I really liked my American Literature class. It wasn't really formal, and the teacher didn't lecture for hours about stuff that no one was interested in. He encouraged discussions of the books, letting us form little work groups within the classroom. We got a chance to talk to other kids and see what they thought about the reading instead of just hearing the teacher's point of view. And when we finished talking in small groups, we were allowed to report to the whole class what we had discussed. Even the regular discussions were good because our teacher really cared about what everyone had to say. We could speak without raising our hands or anything, and he didn't even get mad! That was good because lots of times I wanted to talk. There were a lot of things in the books which I really understood—characters that were like me—and my teacher encouraged me to speak up and share my feelings with the class. He also encouraged good communication between him and the students by having personal writing conferences with individual students on a regular basis. That way, we got to see what he thought about how we were doing in class.

FIGURE 6.9
ELEMENTARY CHECKLIST

Mastery	**Interpersonal**
○ I enjoy doing things I know about.	○ I like games that everyone can play and nobody loses.
○ I'm good at getting things done.	○ I enjoy working with friends.
○ I like copying or making things.	○ I'm good at helping others.
○ I follow a routine every morning.	○ I like group projects.
○ I work out problems step-by-step.	○ I like it when everyone is happy.
	○ I am good at understanding other people's feelings.
Understanding	**Self-Expressive**
○ I enjoy reading about things that interest me.	○ I enjoy doing things I've never done before.
○ I'm good at organizing things.	○ I'm good at discovering things.
○ I like to figure out how things work.	○ I think of lots of new ideas.
○ I learn mostly from reading.	○ I like to use my imagination.
○ I like assignments that make me think.	○ I like art and music.
○ I like to take my time on projects that interest me.	○ I like "What if . . ." questions better than "yes-and-no" questions.

FIGURE 6.10
SAMPLE LEARNING PREFERENCE INVENTORY ITEMS

1. I'm good at

① ② ③ ④ helping others
① ② ③ ④ getting things done
① ② ③ ④ organizing things
① ② ③ ④ discovering things

2. I like questions that ask me

① ② ③ ④ to think of new and original ideas
① ② ③ ④ to explain why things happen
① ② ③ ④ to choose the correct answer
① ② ③ ④ how I feel about things

3. In a group I am usually

① ② ③ ④ quiet
① ② ③ ④ noisy
① ② ③ ④ talkative
① ② ③ ④ listening

4. When I'm making something I prefer to

① ② ③ ④ have someone show me how to do it
① ② ③ ④ follow the directions one step at a time
① ② ③ ④ figure out how to do it myself
① ② ③ ④ find a new way for doing it

Source: From the Hanson-Silver Learning Preference Inventory. Copyright (c) 1991 by Silver Strong & Associates' Thoughtful Education Press.

FIGURE 6.11
SAMPLE VISUALIZATION OF A STUDENT'S PROFILE

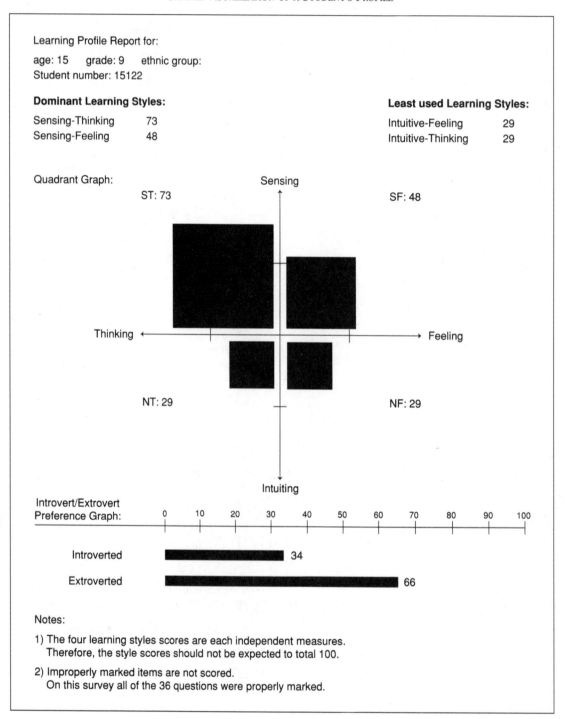

Learning Profile Report for:

age: 15   grade: 9   ethnic group:
Student number: 15122

Dominant Learning Styles:

Sensing-Thinking   73
Sensing-Feeling   48

Least used Learning Styles:

Intuitive-Feeling   29
Intuitive-Thinking   29

Quadrant Graph:

ST: 73   Sensing   SF: 48

Thinking ←   → Feeling

NT: 29   NF: 29

Intuiting

Introvert/Extrovert
Preference Graph: 0   10   20   30   40   50   60   70   80   90   100

Introverted   34

Extroverted   66

Notes:

1) The four learning styles scores are each independent measures.
   Therefore, the style scores should not be expected to total 100.

2) Improperly marked items are not scored.
   On this survey all of the 36 questions were properly marked.

FIGURE 6.12
STYLE AMOEBA

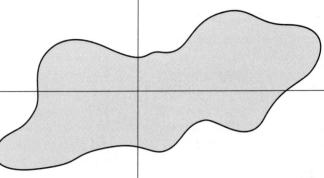

(ST) Brown
Brown is an earthy color. It signifies "down-to-earth" ideas that usually are accepted as simple, factual, and without variance in the answers. It gives a straightforward type of feeling without deviating from the standard. The ST likes things to be "down-to-earth."

(SF) Red
Red often is used to show feelings. It gives an impression of emotion. Red is the significant color for the nation's most "feeling" holiday, Valentine's Day. The SF likes everything to be personalized or have feeling.

(NT) Green
Green is the color of the grass. The grass comes and goes each year and always promotes growth and wonder. Green has come to symbolize this "wonder." It represents a desire to know more and understand why things work. It also means "GO." The NT's thoughts are always on the "go"!

(NF) Purple
Purple is a creative color. It is not a basic color, nor is it a very common one. It gives the impression of uniqueness and individuality in creation or design when applied to art or drawing. Purple is also a color chosen often for its beauty. An NF is constantly striving to make beauty.

Note: ST = Sensing-Thinking learner; SF = Sensing-Feeling learner; NT = Intuitive- Thinking learner; NF = Intuitive-Feeling learner.

Source: Rugg-Davis, J. K. (1994). *Number the stars: A literature resource guide.* St. Louis: Milliken Publishing. Reproduced by permission.

The LPI provides teachers with a comprehensive picture of each student's learning profile, including a visual overview (see Figure 6.11), learning strengths, learning weaknesses, preferred environment, and motivating activities.

Having this information at their disposal, teachers can make informed decisions about how to address student styles so that students are effectively accommodated, challenged, and motivated to grow as learners. Use of the LPI has proven especially beneficial in addressing the needs of underachievers, low achievers, and gifted and talented students.

"Style Amoeba"

A fun and effective method for teaching style to elementary students is to use a "style amoeba" (see Figure 6.12). Used by Janice Rugg-Davis

(1994), a style amoeba is a grid with four style descriptions. The students draw an amoeba in the middle, placing most of the body in the quadrant they feel most expresses their style; they place proportional amounts in each of the remaining quadrants. They then color the sections of the amoeba according to its quadrant.

Other Methods

Another method is to discuss characters students have read or learned about that reflect a particular style. What style is Hamlet? How about Tom Sawyer and Huck Finn? What style is Holden Caulfield from *The Catcher in the Rye*? Do Ralph, Piggy, Jack, and Simon from *Lord of the Flies* each embody a particular learning

FIGURE 6.13–6.16
"STYLE SYMBOLS" DEMO

One style uses the five senses and thinking. The symbol of this style is the hand. We use the hand to symbolize these students because they like to learn through hands-on activities, and they like following directions one step at a time. These learners like to be told or shown what to do; also, they like activities that have right or wrong answers.

A second style likes to learn with the five senses and feelings. The symbol for this style is the heart. We use the heart to represent this style because these students like to learn with their friends. They like to learn about people and how they feel. They like questions that ask about their feelings. They also like to be shown what to do, but like to talk and work with others as they learn.

A third style likes to learn through the sixth sense—intuition—and thinking. The symbol for this style is the head. We use the head to represent this style because these students like to learn by thinking about things. These students like to solve problems and explain things. They enjoy questions that ask them to explain how and why things work.

The last style uses the sixth sense—intuition—along with feeling. The symbol for this style is the eye. We use the eye because these students love to use their imagination to see things that can't be seen by the senses. They like activities that allow them to pretend and to create their own ideas. They also like to choose their own projects and to make things that are new and different.

style? What are the strengths and weaknesses of each character? Or you could talk about any other sources that have characters showing a particular learning style. For example, the characters in the Peanuts comic strip represent all four styles. Charlie Brown is a strong Sensing-Feeling (Interpersonal) thinker. He takes things to heart; he is always concerned about how his friends feel; he goes out of his way to help others. Lucy is a dominant Sensing-Thinking learner (Mastery). She believes in following procedures and she knows there is always a "right" way to do things. Linus is a true Intuitive-Thinking learner (Understanding). He loves to know how things work and explain them to his friends. There is nothing he likes better than a good discussion, and he learns by questioning. Schroeder is a creative Intuitive-Feeling thinker (Self-Expressive). Much of his time is devoted to his music, and he is often in a creative fog.

Another teacher used four symbols to represent each style (see Figures 6.13–6.16).

Reflection Charts

Once your students understand the four styles, they can begin to reflect on how they use each style and what skills they need to develop in order to improve their learning in that style. For example, one way to get students to reflect is to ask them to pay attention to how they went about the task, to decide what styles they used, and to give themselves advice for the next time they complete a task [see Figure 6.17].

Teaching Students About Intelligences

Many of the methods for teaching students about style will also serve as ways to teach them about multiple intelligences. For example, you can assign students tasks that ask them to use different intelligences (rather than styles) and ask them to reflect on their learning process afterward. You can also use student descriptions and case studies that emphasize intelligences rather than styles. Simple intelligence checklists and inventories (like the Multiple Intelligences Indicator in Appendix A) can also be developed, and methods like analyzing characters in literature and history can work well for learning both styles and intelligences. Certainly, examining the accomplishments of famous people (as you did in Chapter 1) will yield a rich lesson on intelligences.

Symbols and Reflection Charts

Using symbols for each intelligence, or asking students to create their own symbols also helps in teaching students about intelligences. It is also a good idea to use a reflection chart to help students pay closer attention to their learning process and to advise themselves on how to improve their learning. Figure 6.18 (p. 98) shows a sample reflection chart.

FIGURE 6.17
STYLE REFLECTION CHART

Noticed	Styles	Advice
I came up with a lot of ideas.	I work well in the Self-Expressive style, but I could do better in Mastery style.	I need to concentrate more on what I'm doing.
I had a hard time selecting which ideas to use.		I need to pay attention to the details.
I worked well with my team.		I need to learn how to decide what to do when
I am a little disorganized.		I have a lot of ideas.

FIGURE 6.18
INTELLIGENCE REFLECTION CHART

Noticed	Styles	Advice
I am creative—I like to use words in strange ways. I like to work by myself. I hum, whistle, and tap a beat while I work.	My linguistic, musical, and intrapersonal intelligences are highly developed. My spatial and logical-mathematical intelligences are somewhat developed. My interpersonal and bodily-kinesthetic intelligences need the most improvement.	I need to "put my guard down" when I work in groups, and I need to listen to others more attentively. I need to begin seeing the way I move and use my body as an intelligence that I can develop.

Demonstration

One way to teach students about the eight intelligences is to ask them to think about things they do or have done that require them to use specific intelligences. After explaining each intelligence, the teacher can stop and engage students in brief activities that demonstrate each intelligence.

For instance, after explaining logical-mathematical intelligence, you might ask students to solve a logic puzzle or make an interpretation of numerical data. Asking students to pay close attention to a piece of music, to use their bodies to represent a concept, to gather and classify natural items, or to work with other students are just some of the many activities you might use to make your demonstration particularly

memorable. Along the way, you can fold in reflection, asking students to note how well they use each intelligence and what they might do to improve.

Intelligence Stations

Another effective method for teaching students about multiple intelligences is to set up intelligence stations or activity centers (Armstrong, 1994). These are learning centers with appropriate activities for each intelligence set up around the classroom. Activity centers can be designed to meet a number of instructional purposes. You might create permanent centers with the same materials at each station all year long and have students explore various topics using these permanent materials. Or you might change the contents of the stations throughout the year so that at the bodily-kinesthetic center, for instance, students can design pyramids using construction blocks while studying Ancient Egypt and later use manipulatives and abacuses to understand math concepts.

To make his stations particularly memorable for students, one teacher chose to use famous people to represent the intelligence of each station. His learning centers were labeled Maya Angelou's Station, Marie Curie's Station, Georgia O'Keeffe's Station, Ludwig von Beethoven's Station, Jackie Joyner-Kersee's Station, Dr. Martin Luther King, Jr.'s Station, Socrates's Station, and Charles Darwin's Station. Before engaging in any activities, students read brief biographical descriptions and, wherever possible, experienced the work of each famous person (e.g., reading a selection of Angelou's poetry, listening to the fourth movement of Beethoven's *Ninth Symphony*, listening to Dr. King's "I Have a Dream" speech). After students had learned about the eight people and their eight intelligences, the class discussed how intelligences are important in helping humans achieve great things.

Conclusion

EARLIER IN THIS BOOK, WHEN WE DISCUSSED curriculum design, we used the metaphor of a house to symbolize renovation, not demolition. We bring it out again because we know teaching is not easy: It takes time, patience, creativity, and plain old hard work. Yet too often it seems teachers are being asked to start all over, to give up some of their autonomy—some of their favorite ideas—and to try something completely new.

Perhaps, then, we should have used the metaphor of the house to stand for teaching in general, rather than for just one component of it. Using multiple intelligences and learning styles to make a better house of teaching does not imply the demolition of older practices, but instead suggests remodeling and improving those practices to increase their power and reach more students. The examples provided by the wonderful teachers whose work we have included in this book prove that some well-considered adjustments make a tremendous difference in the classroom.

Just as important, the house of teaching should also be a place where teachers and students enjoy living. One of the best places to start when deciding how and where to use the ideas from this book is at the "Are-we-having-fun-yet?" rule. Brain research tells us that learning is a natural state and that exploring concepts, discovering new ideas, and making connections are immensely pleasurable and stimulating activities for the human brain. What is too often overlooked in the world of professional development is the idea that when changes feel like changes for their own sake—when they do not seem exciting or inspiring or likely to make learning pleasurable—they are probably not going to lead to positive growth in the classroom.

When we unite learning styles and multiple intelligences, we are uniting the best means at our disposal for bringing all students and all viewpoints to the table in the house of learning. But we are also reminding ourselves again that teaching and learning should be enjoyable experiences. We have seen from the work of teachers like Charlene Larkin, Carl Carrozza, Wendy Ecklund Lambert, Sherry Gibbon, Theodora Lacey, Mary Daley, Robin Cederblad, Susan Daniels, Linda Diskin, and Abigail Silver that style- and intelligence-fair instruction gets students hooked into learning. We can see, in the classrooms of teachers such as Eva Benevento and William Massimo, that using learning styles and intelligences in designing lesson plans makes for powerful and rewarding learning experiences. We can see the power of styles and intelligences in the way students respond so enthusiastically to learning about their own unique learning preferences in classrooms like Sue Ulrey's, Barb Heinzman's, Joanne Curran's, Stacey Gerhardt's, and Janice Rugg-Davis's.

We have even seen from the work of teachers like Claudia Geocaris and Maria Ross how the use of learning styles and multiple intelligences can make testing something students and teachers get excited about. More generally, what these teachers prove is that the integration of learning styles and multiple intelligences gives all students the chance to express themselves, find their hidden talents and callings, and experience the joys of success. This integration should never feel like drudgery or some mechanical process imposed on students. If it does, then we can be certain it is not doing what it is intended or able to do: inspire and empower students to reach their full potentials.

To be sure, there is much more to consider than whether the ideas in this book (or any new ideas, for that matter) are likely to bring pleasure to the educational experience. But it is crucial that we do not lose sight of an ancient wisdom repeatedly reinforced by modern science—one first posed by Aristotle in the fourth century Before the Common Era: "To learn is a natural pleasure, not confined to philosophers, but common to all" (see T. Twining's translation of Aristotle, 1971, p. 1.5).

Multiple Intelligences Indicator for Adults

Verbal-Linguistic

Logical-Mathematical   Interpersonal

Spatial   Naturalist

Musical   Intrapersonal

Bodily-Kinesthetic

A self-diagnostic tool for adults to use in identifying their multiple intelligences profile based on Howard Gardner's Theory of Multiple Intelligences

Multiple Intelligences Indicator

For each of the following behaviors, determine the rating that best describes your behavior:
4 - This applies to me completely.
3 - This applies to me strongly.
2 - This applies to me somewhat.
1 - This hardly applies to me.
0 - This does not apply to me at all.

I

___ A. I enjoy reading.
___ B. I tend to think of logic problems as exciting challenges.
___ C. I sketch or draw when I think.
___ D. I like to sing, even to myself.
___ E. I am good at using my hands to fix or build things.
___ F. I am good at making new friends.
___ G. I like to spend time thinking about myself and what I value.
___ H. I like being outside whenever possible.

II

___ A. When I learn a new vocabulary word, I try to use it in my conversation or writing.
___ B. I prefer math to social studies and English classes.
___ C. I am able to distinguish subtle variations in color, line, and shape.
___ D. I listen to music often.
___ E. I have a good sense of balance and coordination.
___ F. I like social gatherings and activities.
___ G. I greatly value my independence.
___ H. I am good at forecasting changes in natural phenomena (such as the coming of seasons or rain).

III

___ A. I like to argue a point or to explain things.
___ B. I am adept at seeing patterns and anomalies in a situation.
___ C. I am good at visualizing ideas.

___ D. I am able to keep a tune.
___ E. I am able to learn a new dance or sport quickly.
___ F. Going to parties is one of my favorite pastimes.
___ G. I often talk to myself.
___ H. I get involved with ecological problems (e.g., cleaning up beaches, preserving a local park).

IV

___ A. I speak in metaphors and use expressive language.
___ B. I am good at working with numbers and data.
___ C. I am good at reading a map.
___ D. I am able to play a musical instrument well.
___ E. I often talk with my hands.
___ F. I am easy to get to know.
___ G. I regularly reflect upon my assets and liabilities.
___ H. I prefer biology to chemistry.

V

___ A. I am good at using words to describe things.
___ B. I take very little on faith alone.
___ C. When I read, I see the story in my head.
___ D. I can tell when music is flat, off-time, or out of key.
___ E. I look forward to physical activity, even if it is strenuous.
___ F. I look for opportunities to work with and meet new people.
___ G. I like to think things through before I take action.
___ H. I am good at outdoor recreations like hunting, fishing, or bird watching.

Source: Silver, Strong, & Associates, Inc. (SS&A), The Thoughtful Education Press. Phone: 800-962-4432; URL: http://www.silverstrong.com. Developed by Harvey F. Silver and Richard W. Strong. Copyright © 1998 by Silver Strong & Associates, Inc. All rights reserved. Reproduction of any or all pages of this instrument or scoring sheet by any process is unlawful without the written permission of SS&A, Inc.

VI

__ A. I am good at using words to persuade others.

__ B. I am comfortable with abstract ideas.

__ C. When I watch a movie, I focus more on what I see than what I hear.

__ D. I have a "musical library" in my head.

__ E. If I can't move around, I get bored.

__ F. I ask the advice of others when I have a difficult decision to make.

__ G. I regularly need time to myself.

__ H. I have a green thumb.

VII

__ A. I am interested in the meaning of words.

__ B. I have an ability to read and understand charts or diagrams with numbers.

__ C. I am good at matching colors and decorating.

__ D. I like to make up my own tunes and melodies.

__ E. I need to manipulate things with my hands to know how they work.

__ F. I dislike confrontations and try to keep harmony when they occur.

__ G. I like to set personal goals for myself.

__ H. I like to draw or take pictures of natural settings or objects.

VIII

__ A. I find writing enjoyable.

__ B. Current debates and topics in science fascinate me.

__ C. I can stand in one location and visualize things from different locations without moving.

__ D. I am good at keeping a beat.

__ E. I like hands-on activities like woodworking, building models, or sewing.

__ F. I am good at making people feel comfortable.

__ G. I tend to trust my own judgment over the advice of others.

__ H. I like hiking and camping.

IX

__ A. I like going to a bookstore or library to read and research ideas.

__ B. I believe that there is a logical explanation for almost everything.

__ C. I am better at remembering faces than names.

__ D. I have a clearly defined musical taste (I know what I like and what I don't).

__ E. I would rather play a sport than watch it.

__ F. I respond strongly to other people.

__ G. I like being my own boss.

__ H. I feel comfortable and confident outdoors.

X

__ A. I'm good at Scrabble, Boggle, crossword puzzles, or other word games.

__ B. I enjoy games that require tactics and strategy.

__ C. I am good at playing Pictionary, solving mazes, and/or identifying optical illusions.

__ D. I am good at remembering the names of songs.

__ E. I am good at mimicking other people's physical behavior.

__ F. I enjoy getting others to work together.

__ G. I like games that I can play alone, like solitaire or computer games.

__ H. I am good at using the sun and the stars to guide myself in the woods.

SCORING

To determine your comfort with each of the eight intelligences, compute your totals for each letter:

Letter	Type of Intelligence	Item										Total
		I	II	III	IV	V	VI	VII	VIII	IX	X	
A	Verbal-Linguistic											
B	Logical-Mathematical											
C	Spatial											
D	Musical											
E	Bodily-Kinesthetic											
F	Interpersonal											
G	Intrapersonal											
H	Naturalist											

VISUALIZING YOUR PROFILE

In order to visualize the strength of your comfort, plot your score on the scale below:

```
                       0——5——10——15——20——25——30——35——40
```

Verbal-Linguistic	0————————20————————40
Logical-Mathematical	0————————20————————40
Spatial	0————————20————————40
Musical	0————————20————————40
Bodily-Kinesthetic	0————————20————————40
Interpersonal	0————————20————————40
Intrapersonal	0————————20————————40
Naturalist	0————————20————————40

COMFORT LEVEL

32–40 - very comfortable with this type of intelligence
24–31 - comfortable with this intelligence
16–23 - moderately comfortable with this intelligence

8–15 - little comfort with this intelligence
0–7 - no comfort with this intelligence

Source: Silver, Strong, & Associates, Inc. (SS&A), The Thoughtful Education Press. Phone: 800-962-4432; URL: http://www.silverstrong.com. Developed by Harvey F. Silver and Richard W. Strong. Copyright © 1998 by Silver Strong & Associates, Inc. All rights reserved. Reproduction of any or all pages of this instrument or scoring sheet by any process is unlawful without the written permission of SS&A, Inc.

APPENDIX b

Learning Styles Inventory for Adults: Sample Pages

Choosing Self Descriptors

In each of the following twenty-five horizontal sets, rank the four behavioral descriptors in order of: first preference (5), second preference (3), third preference (1), fourth preference (0).

Be sure to assign a different weighted number (5, 3, 1, 0) to each of the four descriptors in each set. Do not make ties. Rank the descriptors according to those which best describe you, i.e., how you approach learning. Note that a rank of zero does

not mean a descriptor does not apply to you; it only means that descriptor is your least preferred.

Please answer every item and keep in mind that there are no right or wrong answers. The aim of this inventory is to describe how you learn, not to evaluate your learning ability or to assign labels. If a set of words is hard to rank at first reading, then go to the next set. Complete the missing set after you've finished all the other items.

> Descriptors are to be analyzed horizontally as sets of four across the lettered columns. Do not compare descriptors vertically.

	A	B	C	D
1.	Creative	Personal	Organized	Analytical
2.	Facts	Formulas	Passions	People
3.	Spontaneous	Flexible	Literal	Interpretive
4.	Harmonize	Question	Utilize	Imagine
5.	Create	Compete	Cooperate	Critique
6.	Remember	Reason	Relate Personally	Reorganize
7.	Discovery	Debate	Directions	Discussion
8.	Patterns	Human Interactions	Details	Possibilities
9.	Feelings	Objects	Ideas	Insights
10.	Action	Wonder	Warmth	Wisdom
11.	Eureka!	Trial & Error	Gut Feeling	Strategy
12.	Realistic	Theoretical	Aesthetic	Humanistic
13.	Specifics	Concepts	Values	Rapport
14.	Logic	Precision	Persuasion	Predictions
15.	Knowing	Relating	Expressing	Understanding
16.	Idealize	Systematize	Socialize	Routinize
17.	Intellectual	Compassionate	Pragmatic	Idealistic
18.	Invention	Intimacy	Information	Inquiry
19.	Loyalties	Rules	Principles	Metaphors
20.	Inspirational	Logical	Experiential	Methodical
21.	Argument	Accuracy	Affiliation	Alternatives
22.	Clarity	Curiosity	Empathy	Originality
23.	Explanation	Extrapolation	Emulation	Example
24.	Enthusiasm	Experience	Effort	Examination
25.	Symmetrical	Sequential	Scientific	Social

Scoring Self Descriptors

To compute your learning score for each of the four learning styles, transfer the numbers from your answer sheet to the scoring sheet. For example, if in the first set of behaviors, you ranked the words as

    1. 0–Creative   5–Personal   3–Organized   1–Analytical

then transfer these numbers to the same words on the scoring sheet, as follows:

    1. 5–Personal   3–Organized   1–Analytical   0–Creative

Compute your scores by adding the numbers for each column vertically.

Scoring Sheet

	S-F Style Sensing-Feeling Rank	S-T Style Sensing-Thinking Rank	N-T Style Intuitive-Thinking Rank	N-F Style Intuitive-Feeling Rank
1.	____Personal	____Organized	____Analytical	____Creative
2.	____People	____Facts	____Formulas	____Passions
3.	____Spontaneous	____Literal	____Interpretive	____Flexible
4.	____Harmonize	____Utilize	____Question	____Imagine
5.	____Cooperate	____Compete	____Critique	____Create
6.	____Relate Personally	____Remember	____Reason	____Reorganize
7.	____Discussion	____Directions	____Debate	____Discovery
8.	____Human Interaction	____Details	____Patterns	____Possibilities
9.	____Feelings	____Objects	____Ideas	____Insights
10.	____Warmth	____Action	____Wisdom	____Wonder
11.	____Gut Feeling	____Trial & Error	____Strategy	____Eureka!
12.	____Humanistic	____Realistic	____Theoretical	____Aesthetic
13.	____Rapport	____Specifics	____Concepts	____Values
14.	____Persuasion	____Precision	____Logic	____Predictions
15.	____Relating	____Knowing	____Understanding	____Expressing
16.	____Socialize	____Routinize	____Systematize	____Idealize
17.	____Compassionate	____Pragmatic	____Intellectual	____Idealistic
18.	____Intimacy	____Information	____Inquiry	____Invention
19.	____Loyalties	____Rules	____Principles	____Metaphors
20.	____Experiential	____Methodical	____Logical	____Inspirational
21.	____Affiliation	____Accuracy	____Argument	____Alternatives
22.	____Empathy	____Clarity	____Curiosity	____Originality
23.	____Emulation	____Example	____Explanation	____Extrapolation
24.	____Experience	____Effort	____Examination	____Enthusiasm
25.	____Social	____Sequential	____Scientific	____Symmetrical

Totals

SF ____   ST ____   NT ____   NF ____

Analyzing Your Learning Preferences

Strengths of the Preferences

100–125	Very strong choice; very comfortable in the style	25–49	Low comfort in the style
75–99	Strong choice; comfortable in the style	0–24	Very low comfort in the style
50–74	Moderate choice		

Learning Profile

No one learning style adequately represents the complexity of one's learning behavior. Everyone operates in a variety of ways in different situations. Depending on how demanding a particular learning challenge may be, one "flexes" or compensates by using other, often less-preferred, styles. It's important, therefore, to identify not just one's dominant or most-accessible style, but also one's entire profile. It is the full profile that gives the only accurate picture of how one functions. One's profile consists of four styles in a descending order of access. The dominant style is the most accessible because it is the most practiced. The auxiliary style is accessible with some additional effort. The third level (tertiary) and least developed (inferior) are such because they are not routinely practiced and, therefore, are much less accessible. One's profile is always a hierarchy, but over time and with increasing consciousness, the tertiary and inferior functions can become more accessible as a result of practice.

MODE	SCORE	STYLE	COMFORT LEVEL
Dominant			
Auxiliary			
Tertiary			
Inferior			

Directions for Plotting Your Learning Profile:

Having completed the scoring of your learning styles, plot your profile below. To plot your profile, mark the score you received for each style on the diagonal line that fits that style. Then connect your marks with a straight line to create a four-sided polygon. This configuration represents a visual presentation of your learning profile.

Visual Presentation of My Learning Profile

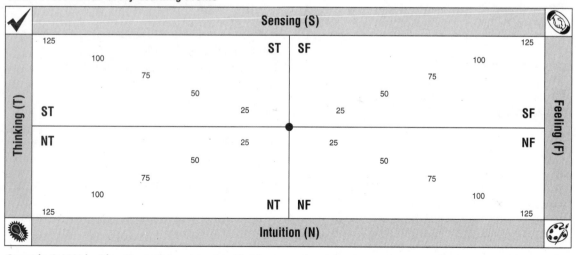

APPENDIX C | The Teaching Strategy Index

Introduction

Using instructional strategies to teach content and skills is not some newfangled idea. Socrates, Aristotle, and St. Thomas Aquinas, among others, all understood the need to teach strategically so as to maximize learning among students. A repertoire of effective teaching strategies is one of the teacher's best means of reaching the full range of learners in the classroom and of making learning deep and memorable for students. There are a number of wonderful resources for developing an array of strategies, including Joyce and Weil's *Models of Teaching* (1996); Silver, Hanson, Strong, and Schwartz's *Teaching Styles and Strategies* (1996); and video programs such as Canter & Associates' *Developing Lifelong Learners* (1996), Video Journal's *Instructional Strategies for Greater Student Achievement* (1995), and ASCD's *Teaching Strategies Library* (1987).

This appendix includes some of our favorite teaching strategies organized by instructional purpose. The learning styles and multiple intelligences that each strategy engages are also provided according to the following keys:

Key to Style (matrixes in column 3):

X = emphasized through the strategy; ✔ = expressed through the strategy:

Sensing-Thinking (Mastery)	Sensing-Feeling (Interpersonal)
Intuitive-Thinking (Understanding)	Intuitive-Feeling (Self-Expressive)

Thus:

$$\frac{X \mid X}{X \mid ✔}$$

means that the particular strategy emphasizes the Mastery, Interpersonal, and Understanding styles and includes an expression of the Self-Expressive style.

Key to Intelligences:

V = verbal-linguistic
L = logical-mathematical

S = spatial
B = bodily-kinesthetic
M = musical

P = interpersonal
I = intrapersonal
N = naturalist.

I. STRATEGIES FOR COLLECTING, ORGANIZING, AND MANAGING INFORMATION

Strategy	Purpose and Description	Style		Multiple Intelligences
New American Lecture	Teacher presents information using a hook, a visual organizer, deep processing, and style questions for processing and maximizing memory.	X	X	V, L, S
		X	X	
COPE	A four-step process for teaching students how to remember information: Collecting, Organizing, Picturing, and Elaborating using memory devices.	X	X	V, L, S, B, M
		X	X	
Main Idea	Students identify keywords used to formulate main ideas and to collect evidence to support them.	X		V, L, S
		X		
Mind's Eye	Students visualize keywords to make predictions, draw pictures, ask questions, or describe feelings before reading a text.		X	V, S, I
			X	
Etch A Sketch	A note-taking device using symbols and discussion of key ideas and important details.	✔	X	V, S, P, I
			X	
Jigsaw	A cooperative learning strategy. Students work in learning teams made up of experts who are responsible for researching subtopics of a larger topic. Experts from each learning team meet to discuss their findings, then return home to their original team to teach their research findings to the group.		X	V, P
		X		
Four-Way Reporting and Recording	A strategy that uses a jigsaw structure and a variety of note-taking devices for collecting and sharing information.	✔	✔	V, L, S, P
		✔	X	
Power Notes	A note-taking device for organizing information according to the power of the ideas recorded.	X		V, L
		X		
Information Search	A reading strategy that begins with a mind map of what students know, establishes questions related to what they want to know, engages them in reading research, and asks them to visually report the new learning.	X	✔	V, L, S, P
		X	✔	

I. Strategies for Collecting, Organizing, and Managing Information—continued

Strategy	Purpose and Description	Style	Multiple Intelligences
Command	Students are taught a skill or procedure on command, one step at a time, by the teacher. The teacher then checks and corrects after each step, guaranteeing 100 percent accuracy.	X	V, B
Proceduralizing	A strategy used to teach the steps in a skill by breaking it down into separate actions and then visualizing and practicing the skill until it becomes automatic.	X	V, S, B
Direct Instruction	Teacher models the skill and provides feedback during directed, guided, and independent practice to help students achieve mastery of the skill.	X	V, L, S, B
Graduated Difficulty	Students assess their level of competence by choosing from an array of tasks at different levels of difficulty, then determine the knowledge and skills they need to practice to advance to the next level.	X ✔	V, L, I
Mastery Review	Students assess their knowledge and skills by reviewing important content. The teacher asks a question and allows students time to respond. The teacher then writes the answer on the board. Students can check their answers immediately or look at the teacher's answer for coaching or guidance. The teacher then reviews the question and answers and continues the process.	X	V, L, I

II. STRATEGIES FOR PROMOTING SOCIAL INTERACTIONS AND GROUP LEARNING

Strategy	Purpose and Description	Style	Multiple Intelligences
Reciprocal Learning	Students work together as peer partners on parallel tasks, one functioning as a "doer," the other as a "guide." The guide provides the doer with clues, encouragement, and feedback to ensure a successful outcome.	X (upper right)	V, P, I
Team Games Tournament	Heterogenous teams are formed to practice previously learned material. Students then compete in homogeneous (three players) tournaments to earn points for their home team.	✔ X (upper left, upper right)	V, P, I
Circle	Students sit in a circle and are invited to share interpersonal information. The leader then asks circle members to review what they heard, to look for similarities and differences, then to draw conclusions about what was shared.	X (upper right), ✔ (lower left)	V, L, P, I
Role Playing	Students assume the identities of others and act out their roles in a scenario. They then reflect on how others think about issues and conflicts, resulting in improved understanding and empathy toward the position of others.	X (upper right), ✔ X (lower left, lower right)	V, P, I
I Teach, You Teach	The class is broken up into threes. One person is assigned as "teacher" from each group. The student teachers meet with the lead teacher, who introduces the new learning to the group while the remaining partners practice previously taught material. The student teachers then return to their groups of three and provide input to the other students. The group is then given a task to assess the group's mastery of the subject.	X X (upper left, upper right)	V, L, S, I, P

III. Strategies for Reasoning, Analysis, and Problem Solving

Strategy	Purpose and Description	Style	Multiple Intelligences
Circle of Knowledge	A discussion strategy built around a sparking activity and a focus question. Students kindle responses individually and in small groups, then participate in a whole-class discussion. The teacher uses a variety of techniques to orchestrate the discussion, maintain focus, and enhance the quality and depth of thought.	top-right: X; bottom-left: X, bottom-right: ✔	V, L, P, I
Compare and Contrast	This strategy moves through three phases: The first asks students to describe objects or ideas using specific criteria; the second focuses on discrimination, comparing, and contrasting using a visual organizer; and the third is a discussion phase that focuses on communicating conclusions.	top-left: ✔, top-right: ✔; bottom-left: X, bottom-right: ✔	V, L, S
Concept Attainment	Concepts are taught by providing examples and non-examples of concepts. Students use the examples to identify critical attributes. Once students have determined the attributes for concepts, they generate their own examples.	top-left: ✔; bottom-left: X, bottom-right: ✔	V, L
Inductive Learning	Students use the classification process of grouping and labeling data to formulate hypotheses, which they then test by finding evidence to support or refute using texts or experiments.	bottom-left: X, bottom-right: X	V, L
Mystery	Students are introduced to a question that puzzles and teases, along with clues needed to explain the mystery. They then organize and interpret clues to build an explanation.	bottom-left: X	V, L
Inquiry	The strategy begins with a discrepant event. Students collect data using "yes" and "no" questions and generate a hypothesis to explain the discrepant event.	bottom-left: X	V, L
Socratic Seminar	Students are given a series of readings and a set of focus questions. The students then take notes and come together for a focused discussion. The lesson culminates with an essay-writing assessment.	top-left: ✔, top-right: ✔; bottom-left: X	V, L., P, I
Do You Hear What I Hear?	Students listen to a rigorous text twice: The first time to get the gist of the reading; the second time to record notes addressing specific questions. Students then meet in small groups to discuss the text. After the discussion, they prepare a retelling of the text.	top-left: ✔, top-right: ✔; bottom-left: X, bottom-right: ✔	V, S, P, I

IV. STRATEGIES FOR THINKING CREATIVELY AND APPLYING WHAT YOU KNOW AND UNDERSTAND

Strategy	Purpose and Description	Style	Multiple Intelligences
Metaphorical Problem Solving	Students use three types of metaphors—direct analogies, personal analogies, and compressed conflicts—to make the familiar strange or to make the strange familiar.	(bottom-right: X)	V, S, P, I
Divergent Thinking	Students generate a variety of responses to an open-ended question or problem. They strive for fluency, creativity, flexibility, and problem solving skills. The goal is to develop an original perspective on the problem.	(bottom-left: X, bottom-right: X)	(All intelligences, depending on content)
Extrapolation	Students extract the structure from one content and apply the same structure to another. This strategy helps students to think beyond the classroom and apply what they learn to everyday living.	(bottom-right: X)	(All intelligences, depending on content)
Knowledge by Design	All knowledge has a design. It has a structure and a purpose and can be analyzed for its advantages and disadvantages, then modified to improve its use. This strategy asks students to improve an existing design, object, or process.	(bottom-right: X)	L, S, I
Task Rotation	Four tasks are centered around a single topic, one in each learning style. Students may choose to complete some tasks or they may be required to complete all four. Tasks may follow an order or may be done at random.	(top: X X, bottom: X X)	(All intelligences, depending on content)
Menus	A combination of Graduated Difficulty and Task Rotation. Students are given an opportunity to choose from a menu of 12 tasks, one in each style and at three levels of difficulty. Students have to choose four tasks, one in each style, and one for each level of difficulty.	(top: X X, bottom: X X)	(All intelligences, depending on content)

References

Aristotle. (1971). *Treatise on poetics* (T. Twining, Trans.). New York: Garland Publishing.

Armstrong, T. (1994). *Multiple intelligences in the classroom.* Alexandria, VA: Association for Supervision and Curriculum Development.

Association for Supervision and Curriculum Development. (1987). *Teaching strategies library* [Videotape]. Alexandria, VA: Author.

Bloom, B. (Ed.). (1956). *Taxonomy of education objectives, the classification of educational goals: Handbook I: Cognitive domain.* New York: David McKay.

Briggs-Myers, I. (1993). *Introduction to type* (5th ed.). Palo Alto, CA: Consulting Psychologists Press.

Brown, A. L. (1989). Analogical learning and transfer: What develops? In I. S. Vosniadov & A. Ortony (Eds.), *Similarity and analogical reasoning.* Cambridge, MA: Cambridge University Press.

Brownlie, F., & Silver, H. F. (1995, January). *Mind's eye.* Paper presented at the seminar "Responding Thoughtfully to the Challenge of Diversity," Delta School District Conference Center, Delta, British Columbia, Canada.

Butler, K. (1984). *Learning and teaching style in theory and practice.* Columbia, CT: The Learner's Dimension.

Caccamo, K. (1998, July 28). Class on learning helps Libertyville kids succeed. *Daily Herald,* Section 5, p. 3.

Canter & Associates. (1996). *Developing lifelong learners* [Videotape]. Santa Monica, CA: Canter & Associates.

Carbo, M. (1992, January-February). Giving unequal learners an equal chance: A reply to a biased critique of learning styles. *Remedial & Special Education, 13*(1), 19–29.

Carrozza, C. (1996). Using learning styles and multiple intelligences to differentiate instruction and assessment. In R. W. Strong & H. F. Silver, *An introduction to thoughtful curriculum & assessment* (pp. 145–152). Woodbridge, NJ: The Thoughtful Education Press.

Collier, J. L., & Collier, C. (1989). *My brother Sam is dead.* New York: Scholastic Paperbacks.

Csikszentmihalyi, M. (1990). *Flow: The psychology of optimal experience.* New York: HarperCollins.

Dunn, R., Griggs, S. A., & Beasley, M. (1995, July). A meta-analytic validation of the Dunn and Dunn model of learning style preferences. *The Journal of Educational Research, 88*(6), 353–362.

Escondido School District. (1979). *Mind's eye.* Escondido, CA: Board of Education.

Gardner, H. (1983). *Frames of mind: The theory of multiple intelligences.* New York: Basic Books.

Gardner, H. (1987). Symposium on the theory of multiple intelligences. In J. C. Bishop, J. Lochhead, & D. N. Perkins (Eds.), *Thinking: The second international conference* (pp. 77–101). Hillsdale, NJ: Lawrence Erlbaum.

Gardner, H. (1995, November). Reflections on multiple intelligences: Myths and messages. *Phi Delta Kappan, 77*(3), 202–209.

Gardner, H. (1997, September). Multiple intelligences as a partner in school improvement. *Educational Leadership, 55*(1), 20–21.

Gardner, H. (1999a). *The disciplined mind: What all students should understand.* New York: Simon & Schuster.

Gardner, H. (1999b). *Intelligence reframed: Multiple intelligences for the 21st century.* New York: Basic Books.

Geocaris, C., & Ross, M. (1999, September). A test worth taking. *Educational Leadership, 57*(1), 29–33.

Glasser, W. (1985). *Control theory*. New York: HarperCollins.

Goodlad, J. I. (1984). *A place called school*. New York: McGraw-Hill.

Gregorc, A. (1985). *Inside styles: Beyond the basics*. Maynard, MA: Gabriel Systems.

Hanson, J. R., & Dewing, T. (1990). *Research on the profiles of at-risk learners: Research monograph series*. Moorestown, NJ: Institute for Studies in Analytic Psychology.

Hanson, J. R., & Silver, H. F. (1991). *The Hanson-Silver Learning Preference Inventory*. Woodbridge, NJ: The Thoughtful Education Press.

Jensen, E. (1996). *Completing the puzzle: The brain-compatible approach to learning*. Del Mar, CA: The Brain Store, Inc.

Joyce, B. R., & Weil, M. (1996). *Models of teaching* (5th ed.). Boston: Allyn & Bacon.

Jung, C. (1923). *Psychological types* (H. G. Baynes, Trans.). New York: Harcourt, Brace & Co.

Lambert, W. E. (1997, September). From Crockett to Tubman: Investigating historical perspectives. *Educational Leadership, 55*, 51–54.

Mager, R. F., & McCann, J. (1963). *Learner-controlled instruction*. Palo Alto, CA: Varian Press.

Mamchur, C. (1996). *A teacher's guide to cognitive type theory and learning style*. Alexandria, VA: Association for Supervision and Curriculum Development.

Martin, C. R. (1997). *Looking at types and careers*. Gainesville, FL: Center for Applications of Psychological Type.

Marzano, R. J. (1992). *A different kind of classroom: Teaching with dimensions of learning*. Alexandria, VA: Association for Supervision and Curriculum Development.

Marzano, R. J., Brandt, R. S., Hughes, C. S., Jones, B. F., Presseisen, B. Z., Rankin, S. C., & Suhor, C. (1988). *Dimensions of thinking: A framework for curriculum and instruction*. Alexandria, VA: Association for Supervision and Curriculum Development.

McCarthy, B. (1982). *The 4mat system*. Arlington Heights, IL: Excel Publishing.

Mosston, M. (1972). *Teaching: From command to discovery*. Belmont, CA: Wadsworth Publishing.

Myers, I. B. (1962). *The Myers-Briggs Type Indicator*. Palo Alto, CA: Consulting Psychologists Press.

Perkins, D., Jay, E., & Tishman, S. (1993, January). Beyond abilities: A dispositional theory of thinking. *Merrill-Palmer Quarterly, 39*(1), 1–21.

Reich, R. B. (1992). *The work of nations: Preparing ourselves for 21st century capitalism*. New York: Random House.

Rugg-Davis, J. K. (1994). *Number the stars: A literature resource guide*. St. Louis: Milliken Publishing.

Silver, H. F., & Hanson, J. R. (1998). *Learning styles and strategies* (3rd ed.). Woodbridge, NJ: The Thoughtful Education Press.

Silver, H. F., Hanson, J. R., Strong, R. W., & Schwartz, P. B. (1996). *Teaching styles and strategies* (3rd ed.). Woodbridge, NJ: The Thoughtful Education Press.

Silver, H., Strong, R., & Commander, J. (1998). *Tools for promoting active, in-depth, learning*. Woodbridge, NJ: The Thoughtful Education Press.

Silver, H., Strong, R., & Perini, M. (1997, September). Integrating learning styles and multiple intelligences. *Educational Leadership, 55*(1), 22–27.

Strong, R. (Keynote). (1999). Simple and deep: Helping students achieve on the new assessments. *National conference on standards and assessment* [Conference]. At the National School Conference Institute, Las Vegas, Nevada.

Suchman, J. R. (1966). *Developing inquiry*. Chicago: Science Research Associates.

Video Journal of Education. (1995). *Instructional strategies for greater student achievement* [Videotape]. Salt Lake City: LPD Video Journal of Education.

Vygotsky, L. S. (1978). *Mind in society*. Cambridge, MA: Harvard University Press.

Wiggins, G. P. (1993). *Assessing student performance: Exploring the purpose and limits of testing*. San Francisco: Jossey-Bass.

Index

About the Authors

Harvey F. Silver, President of Silver Strong & Associates, was recently named as one of the 100 most influential teachers in the United States. He is the coauthor of numerous books for educators, including the best-selling Teaching Styles and Strategies, which is currently being used in the Master of Arts in Teaching (MAT) programs at 14 colleges and universities. Harvey is a member of the advisory board of the International Creative and Innovative Thinking Association.

Richard W. Strong is Vice President of Silver Strong & Associates and has served as a trainer/consultant to hundreds of school districts around the world. As cofounder of the Institute for Community and Difference, Richard has been studying democratic teaching practices in public and private schools for more than 10 years. Richard has written and developed several educational books and products, including *Questioning Styles and Strategies* for the Thoughtful Education Press and the *Teaching Strategies Video Library* for ASCD.

Matthew J. Perini, the Director of Publishing at Silver Strong & Associates, has authored curriculum guides, articles, and research studies on a wide range of topics, including learning styles, multiple intelligences, and effective teaching practices. With Harvey Silver and Richard Strong, Matthew is the coauthor of *Discovering Nonfiction: Twenty-five Powerful Teaching Strategies, Grades 2–8.*

Contact Harvey Silver and Richard Strong at
   Silver Strong & Associates, Inc.
   941 Whitehorse Ave.
   Trenton, NJ 08610
   Phone: 609-581-1900
   Fax: 609-581-5360
   E-mail: Harvey Silver
      (hsilver@silverstrong.com)
      Richard Strong
      (rstrong@silverstrong.com)

Contact Matthew Perini at
   Silver Strong & Associates, Inc.
   334 Kinderkamack Rd.
   Oradell, NJ 07649
   Phone: 201-225-9090
   Fax: 201-225-9024
   E-mail: Matthew Perini
      (mperini@silverstrong.com)

Related ASCD Resources:
Learning Styles and Multiple Intelligences

Audiotapes

How Multiple Intelligences and Learning Style Fit: The Research and Practical Applications (stock no. 298137)

How to Improve Student Achievement on the New State Performance Assessments with Harvey Silver and Richard Strong (stock no. 299248; part of a set from the 1999 ASCD Conference)

Multiple Assessments for Multiple Intelligences by Beth Swartz (stock no. 296267)

On Multiple Intelligences and Education by Howard Gardner (stock no. 295056)

Teaching to Different Learning Styles and Multiple Intelligences with Harvey Silver and Richard Strong (stock no. 296042)

Teaching Thinking to Multiple Intelligences and Diverse Student Populations by Richard Strong (stock no. 294022)

CD-ROM

Exploring Our Multiple Intelligences (stock no. 596276)

Online Course

Multiple Intelligences Professional Development Online course (http://www.ascd.org/pdi/pd.html)

Print Products

ASCD Topic Pack— *Multiple Intelligences* (stock no. 198220)

Becoming a Multiple Intelligences School by Thomas R. Hoerr (stock no. 100006) (see also Videotapes)

Marching to Different Drummers (2nd ed.) by Pat Burke Guild and Stephen Garger (stock no. 198186)

Multiple Intelligences and Student Achievement: Success Stories from Six Schools by Linda Campbell and Bruce Campbell (stock no. 199274)

Multiple Intelligences in the Classroom (1st ed., in Spanish) by Thomas Armstrong (stock no. 895211H17)

Multiple Intelligences in the Classroom (2nd ed.) by Thomas Armstrong (stock no. 100041)

Videotapes

Becoming a Multiple Intelligences School, Books in Action Video Series (Video only: stock no. 400213; 10 copies of book plus video: stock no. 700218)

The Multiple Intelligences Series by Bruce and Linda Campbell (stock no. 495003)

The Teaching Strategies Library with Richard Strong, Harvey Silver, and Robert Hanson (stock no. 614178)

Video Library of Teaching Episodes with Harvey Silver, Richard Strong, Pat Wolfe, Keith Atcheson (24 episodes, various stock nos.)

For more information, visit us on the World Wide Web (**http://www.ascd.org**), send an e-mail message to member@ascd.org, call the ASCD Service Center (1-800-933-ASCD or 703-578-9600, then press 2), send a fax to 703-575-5400, or write to Information Services, ASCD, 1703 N. Beauregard St., Alexandria, VA 22311-1714 USA.